This is Homeschooling

The number of homeschooling families has grown in recent years, along with the number of methods for learning at home. In this timely book, you'll meet diverse families that are engaging in the day-to-day work of a variety of approaches, including self-directed learning, unschooling, nature-based education, farmschooling, wildschooling, and worldschooling.

Chapters and interludes are written by scholars and families engaged in this work, who show how their approaches take a balanced, slower-paced, and nature-minded approach to learning, nourishing the child's heart and brain. They also address common critiques of homeschooling and show how it is something that can be normalized and encouraged as a positive educational tool, helping families bond and live life to the fullest. Each chapter includes practical applications you can use right away in your own journey.

Simultaneously inspirational and practical, this book will help guide and motivate those who are either considering or already homeschooling to see the possibilities of what learning and education can truly be.

Katie Rybakova Mathews is a city-turned-country girl with a Ph.D. in Curriculum and Instruction from Florida State University. She is an Associate Professor of Education at Thomas College and owns a homestead with her husband Eddie where they are raising two girls in the beautiful state of Maine along with Nigerian Dwarf goats and Salmon Faverolles chickens. Her expertise lies in literacy, technology, and young adult literature.

With contributors Nicolette Sowder, Hunter Clarke-Fields, Joel Salatin, Robert Kunzman, Ginny Yurich, Gina Riley, Ben Riley, Robyn Robledo, Monet Poe, George Kaponay, Michael R. Barnes, Nicki Farrell, Vicci Oliver, and Alyson Long.

This is Homeschooling

Stories of Unconventional Learning Practices On the Road and In Nature

Edited by Katie Rybakova Mathews

Routledge
Taylor & Francis Group

NEW YORK AND LONDON

Cover image: © Getty images

First published 2023
by Routledge
605 Third Avenue, New York, NY 10158

and by Routledge
4 Park Square, Milton Park, Abingdon, Oxon, OX14 4RN

Routledge is an imprint of the Taylor & Francis Group, an informa business

© 2023 Katie Rybakova Mathews

Library of Congress Cataloging-in-Publication Data
Names: Rybakova Mathews, Katie, editor.
Title: This is homeschooling : stories of unconventional learning practices on the road and in nature / edited by Katie Rybakova Mathews.
Description: New York, NY : Routledge, 2022. | Includes bibliographical references. |
Identifiers: LCCN 2022001523 (print) | LCCN 2022001524 (ebook) | ISBN 9781032212210 (hardback) | ISBN 9781032201405 (paperback) | ISBN 9781003267362 (ebook)
Subjects: LCSH: Home schooling.
Classification: LCC LC40 .T45 2022 (print) | LCC LC40 (ebook) | DDC 371.01/2--dc23/eng/20220207
LC record available at https://lccn.loc.gov/2022001523
LC ebook record available at https://lccn.loc.gov/2022001524

ISBN: 978-1-032-21221-0 (hbk)
ISBN: 978-1-032-20140-5 (pbk)
ISBN: 978-1-003-26736-2 (ebk)

DOI: 10.4324/9781003267362

Typeset in Palatino
by SPi Technologies India Pvt Ltd (Straive)

To Anastasia and Nadejda—when you reach for the stars, don't forget to enjoy the view.

Contents

Editor

Katie Rybakova Mathews is a city-turned-country girl with a Ph.D. in Curriculum and Instruction from Florida State University. She is an Associate Professor of Education at Thomas College and owns a homestead with her husband Eddie. Her and Eddie are raising two girls in the beautiful state of Maine along with Nigerian Dwarf goats and Salmon Faverolles chickens. Her expertise lies in literacy, technology, and young adult literature.

Contributors

Michael R. Barnes is currently a postdoctoral researcher at the University of Minnesota Twin Cities. His work specializes in utilizing interdisciplinary approaches to understand complex socio-ecological systems and sits at the intersection of psychology, sustainability, and design.

Hunter Clarke-Fields, MSAE, RYT, is a mindful mama mentor. Hunter is the creator of the Mindful Parenting course, host of the Mindful Mama podcast and widely-followed author of *Raising Good Humans: A Mindful Guide to Breaking the Cycle of Reactive Parenting and Raising Kind, Confident Kids*. She helps parents bring calm and peace into their daily lives. Hunter has over twenty years of experience in meditation practices and has taught mindfulness to thousands worldwide.

Nicki Farrell is the co-founder and director of Wildlings Forest School and is a high school English and outdoor recreation teacher. Raised on a farm in remote South Australia, Nicki's favorite childhood memories are of family camping trips, climbing trees, hiding amongst wool bales and rock-hopping over rock pools. Nicki is married to online triathlon coach and ex-teacher Scott Farrell and they have two children (boys) aged seven and nine years.

In 2009 **George Kaponay** traded an 80-hour work week for the bliss of family life, and along with his wife Bobi, and their twins (girl/boy) Réka and Lalika, started a learning adventure which, over the course of the last thirteen years, has seen them live, learn, grow, and appreciate the people, cultures, and customs of 52 countries on six continents.

Robert Kunzman is Professor of Curriculum Studies and Philosophy of Education at Indiana University, and the Managing Director of the International Center for Home Education Research (ICHER). He is the author of more than two dozen publications about homeschooling, including *Write These Laws on Your Children: Inside the World of Conservative Christian Homeschooling* (Beacon, 2009).

Alyson Long is the creator of World Travel Family travel blog and is a full-time traveler, blogger, and travel writer. She has a B.Sc. and worked in pathology before entering the travel arena. World Travel Family Travel Blog has been helping others travel more, better, and further since 2012, when Alyson and James first had this life-changing idea. On this site you can find endless travel information, tips, and guides plus how to travel, how to fund travel, and how to start your own travel blog.

Vicci Oliver is co-founder and director of Wildings Forest School, a marine biologist, and a high school science teacher. The ocean has always been home for Vicci. Living in South East Queensland has been the perfect backdrop for a life of adventure chasing dolphins and whales on a mission to spread love for the natural world. After spending a few years teaching in traditional schools, Vicci's world was soon opened to alternative models of learning, particularly the Forest School and unschooling philosophies. Vicci is married to builder, Jamie Oliver, and they have two children (girls) aged seven and nine years.

Monet Poe is an artist, a soul guide for youth and families, and an eternal student. Raised between Charleston SC and a nomadic life, she and her mom chose a path of radical homeschooling. Her first business was at nine selling her art and face painting at the farmer's market. She and her mother Sarah co-created Poes for Peace where she supports parents in understanding their child's unique genius so that all children may be honored for who they came here to be as well as connecting young adults with their soul's purpose. She spends most of her days painting with watercolors and playing with her beloved dog Luna.

Ben Riley, M.A. is a musician, music educator, writer, editor, and researcher who was unschooled for his entire school years. Ben has written and edited numerous scholarly and journalistic articles, book chapters, and encyclopedia entries that have been published by Grey House Publishing, IGI Global, *Life Learning Magazine, The Envoy, The Fine Print, The Journal of Unschooling and Alternative Learning*, and *Tipping Points Magazine*. As an educator, Ben utilizes a personalized approach which considers the unique needs and abilities of each student. His research focuses on music, education, and self-directed learning.

Gina Riley, Ph.D. is a clinical professor and Program Leader of the Adolescent Special Education Program at CUNY – Hunter College. Dr. Riley has over fifteen years' experience working with teens diagnosed with learning disabilities and emotional/behavioral disorders. She is also a seasoned academic, with years of teaching, research, and supervisory experience within the fields of special education, psychology, school psychology, and mental health counseling. In addition, Dr. Riley has extensive experience in online education and distance learning at the college/university level. She is known internationally for her work in the fields of homeschooling, unschooling, and self-directed learning. Her books include *Unschooling: Exploring Learning Beyond The Classroom* (Palgrave Macmillan, 2020) and *The Homeschooling Starter Guide* (Rockridge Press, 2021).

Robyn Robledo helps people break free of their programming and subconscious thought patterns to create new belief systems that empower them to chase their passions and live their purpose. You can learn more about coaching at http://robynrobledo.com. Robyn also runs two websites with her daughters— nomad-swithapurpose.com and makingmindfulnessfun.com

Joel Salatin and his family own and operate Polyface Farm in Virginia's Shenandoah Valley. He is editor of *Stockman Grass Farmer* magazine and has written fifteen books on non-chemical farming, culture, and family business. He writes a monthly column in the magazine *Plain Values*, a weekly column in the online magazine *Manward*, and does presentations around the world on food, farming, and family business.

Nicolette Sowder is the founder of Wilder Child and wildschooling, representing one of the largest global, online communities of nature-connected parents and educators. Her experience as a teacher in a traditional classroom strengthened her resolve to help design nature-bonded, visceral learning experiences outside of those four walls. She is committed to furthering the outdoor education movement through her work as an educator at Strong Roots Natural Learning Community. She finds her center, inspiration and a lot of eggs on her 60-acre farmstead in Michigan where she wildschools her two daughters.

Ginny Yurich is a Michigan mother of five and the founder of the global 1000 Hours Outside™ movement. Many people from all walks of life look to her for inspiration as well as practical tips on how to put down the screens and get outside. Ginny has a master's degree in education from the University of Michigan and she loves growing zinnias. She is the author of *The 1000 Hours Outside Activity Book* and *The Little Farmhouse in West Virginia*.

The editor would also like to extend a special thank you to **Linda McGurk** and **Dr. Peter Gray**, who are interviewed in the book, and **Isabelle Robledo**, whose poem is featured.

Acknowledgments

This book would have never come to fruition without the unwavering support of my husband, Eddie. He has served as my editor, my advisor, my support, my rock, and my inspiration. I cannot wait to take this homeschooling journey with you. I would also like to thank my mom and dad for teaching me that what is right is not always what is popular, and that if I use my brain and my intuition, I can accomplish great things. Without my two daughters this book wouldn't have existed. Starting with the chain of events that lead to this publication in your hands, it is my hope and dream to provide the best education possible. I want to thank David and Pamela for winning the award for most supportive in-laws. Editor Lauren and the entire Routledge team were amazing, supportive, and made my first book project so easy and filled with joy. I could not have asked for a better team.

Speaking of team, this book would not have had the same impact without the phenomenal contributors. Thank you for answering my call, supporting the homeschooling community, and inspiring my own journey Joel, Nicolette, Monet, Nicki, Linda, Robert, Peter, Ginny, Gina, Ben, Robin, Alyson, George, Michael, Hunter, and Isabella. You all are amazing humans.

Preface

A Battle Cry from the Homeschooling Community

My 3-year-old crouches down by a squash flower in our garden, exclaiming like only a toddler can: "Mama, look! Honeybee!" I squat down next to her, and refrain from telling her about the pollination methods of the honeybee, which is, frankly, so hard, because I am itching to "educate" her. My head spins with the possibilities. Let's talk about hexagons, nature's strongest shape—the shape of which honeycombs are made. We can direct that into a math lesson eventually. We can also talk about how bees communicate with each other, and how that can be a language just like we speak English and Russian at home. On and on my adult brain carries on, thankfully wordlessly. Because see, if I did follow through on this "education," what I would be doing is ruining the magic. My daughter is still mesmerized by this gentle, buzzing insect. Education, in this moment, has nothing to do with what I can tell her about bees.

It is no wonder that my instinct was not to revel in the magic but instead make it a "teachable moment". After all, I myself have been trained by the system—all the way, actually, meaning I have a doctorate in curriculum and instruction. Ironically, my education, paired with voracious reading, experience, and observations, have led me *away* from traditional public schooling with a scripted curriculum and instead toward a more balanced, slower-paced, and nature-minded approach to learning. After all, like Nicolette Sowder, founder of the wildschooling philosophy, has said: "Mother nature is the third parent" (2018, np).

When we live in a world of what Marc Prensky (2014) calls VUCA—rife with volatility, uncertainty, complexity, and ambiguity—we cannot expect a standardized and scripted curriculum to produce creative, unstandardized adults. We cannot expect teachers to do the job they are meant to do creatively and autonomously if we hand them a scripted curriculum. We cannot expect our children to grow up understanding that success is more than just the money you make and the number of degrees you have if we do not first model this ourselves, parenting and educating with conviction, caring, and compassion. What I see in many early elementary classrooms frightens me—little CEOs-in-training are diligently finishing the scripted curriculum (often silently at their desks) at the expense of their current and future mental health. The ones that cannot sit still are labeled neuro-atypical and flooded with acronyms (i.e., IEP, 504, ADHD, ADD), frustrating both child and parent. The kids are not okay. This is not an indictment on teachers—often, teachers are shackled by politics much larger and more menacing than the classroom level. Building administrators are as strapped by these politics as the instructors.

Other scholars see this alarming phenomenon as well. Borba (2021), in addition to chronicling how wealthy parents seek out college prep for their *pre-Kindergarten-aged* children, wrote starkly of kids' inability to thrive and failure to launch:

> Forty percent of young adults—a seventy-five-year-record high—live with parents or relatives. Serious psychological distress, including feelings of anxiety and hopelessness, jumped 71 percent among eighteen to twenty-five-year-olds from 2008 to 2017; depression surged 69 percent among sixteen-to seventeen-year-olds. Beware: a crisis like the pandemic exacerbates preexisting stress and mental health issues.
>
> (p. 50)

Sir Ken Robinson spoke of the diminishing divergent and creative thinking of kindergarten students as they move through middle school and high school along with the diminishing emphasis on arts and humanities—instead of couching education in the aesthetics of the world, "we get them through school by anesthetizing them." Countless homeschooling parents, from Julie Bogart (author of *The Brave Learner*) to Ainsley Arment (author of *The Call of the Wild and Free*), share their accounts of their children's brief stints in traditional schooling. Arment wrote of her eldest son's kindergarten experience:

> His disposition toward us changed. He seemed more distant. He became more interested in what other kids thought of him. He was losing his childlike innocence. I saw the light go out of his eyes…it didn't seem right that strangers got to spend more time with my son than I did.
>
> (p. 4)

Dr. Peter Gray, a research professor of psychology at Boston College and author of *Free to Learn* (Gray, 2013), wrote about the artificially created judgment and competition inherent in traditional public schooling structures, along with the importance of play (we will read more of his thoughts in a subsequent chapter in this book). Evolutionary biologists Heying and Weinstein (2021) further accentuated Gray's point by recognizing that our school system uses metrics like "how much, how fast, how well" (p. 170) vs. helping young people grapple with questions like "Who am I, and what am I going to do about it?" (p. 171). The scholars do not mince words: "For children, school can be understood as love and parenting commodified" (p. 170) and recognize that a deep paradigm shift is necessary both in modern education and modern parenting to avoid the creation of citizens who have developed learned helplessness versus wisdom.

We are a society so fraught with competition and metrics of "how much and how fast" that it has weaved its way into the practices of parenting and educating our children. No one wins a medal or gets a bonus if their child walks at 10 months old, but somehow, we feel guilty that our child walks at 14 months old. No one gets brownie points if their child reads at 3.5, nor does the world stop if our 7-year-old does not yet read.

Yet as education becomes more standardized, those off of the roadmap of expectation are at best labeled gifted and talented, destined for an Ivy League education, and at worst labeled as learning-disabled, which is not only detrimental to their now-limited educational pathways but also just plain confusing and frustrating for child and parent alike. In a later chapter we'll meet Monet Poe, who wrote a searing and passionate chapter geared toward the damaging effects of such labels. What do we expect of a child who is told they are somehow not normal when they try to fare in "normal" classroom activities, only to succumb to self-fulfilling prophecy? When did skipping recess for an extra block of literacy worksheets become normal?

It is no wonder, then, why droves of families pushed into homeschooling by the pandemic are choosing to continue (McShane, 2021), and why homeschooling is becoming secular and diversified. According to the National Home Education Research Institute (2021), the number of homeschooling families ballooned from 2.5 million in the spring of 2019 to 4.5–5.0 million in spring, 2021. With growing numbers come differentiated methods of "doing school" at home. As book chapter authors Nicki and Vicci quip, it should be called "not-at-home schooling." Many homeschooling families do purchase curriculum or abide by a stricter guideline of school rhythm such as the Charlotte Mason approach (her two major points were spending 4–6 hours outside and copy work, both of which have inspired modernized versions such as Ginny Yurich's *1000 Hours Outside* movement— another fantastic author we'll learn from in this book).

However, an increasing number of families are searching for stories of those using minimal curriculum, creating their own curriculum, or not using any curriculum at all. Niche approaches such as roadschooling, worldschooling, wildschooling, unschooling, and nature-based education are gaining popularity because they do not silo formal academic education from learning about life. The focus of these kinds of "curriculum" is on life balance— nourishing the child's heart as well as their brain. Balance. We are exiting the go-go-go world and seeking balance for our children and ourselves.

Part of seeking balance means seeking ways in which to promote it. That was the impetus for writing this book. I have read countless books on homeschooling and education. I wanted more stories. Heying and Weinstein (2021) wrote that storytelling is one of our most primal ways of knowledge-making as a human species. We have made an art out of dining and learning together, whether over a real or proverbial fire.

In this book, you'll meet diverse families who are engaging in the day-to-day work of a variety of approaches, including unschooling, nature-based education, farmschooling (from none other than *the* Joel Salatin), wildschooling, and worldschooling. Many of these philosophies overlap and work off of each other, and there is no "right" way of doing any of them. I invite you to sit over the proverbial fire with us, so that you may begin to contemplate how your story contributes to the tapestry that is homeschooling.

The book is combined into three sections split by interludes written by scholars in various fields. There are pieces of poetry and artwork throughout the text meant to inspire and showcase what homeschoolers and their families can accomplish together. In the first section we will meet families engaging in unschooling and farmschooling, followed by nature-based educators in section two and worldschoolers in section three, and throughout all there are elements of a variety of philosophies integrated across families' stories. This underscores that these educational philosophies do not stand alone and are not meant to be followed like doctrine. Ultimately, these methods, and the subsequent stories in this book, are meant to help us all embrace what learning and education *could* be. Each chapter has either a separate section specific to *doing something* (applicably titled *Do Something*) or has an integrated practical application to take away and use right away in your own journey.

Taken together, these chapters form more than a cohesive, albeit diverse, narrative; they are a battle cry from the homeschooling community. They are a passionate and confident reply to those labelling us homeschoolers as renegades, and a powerful call to everyone that it is time we normalize and encourage homeschooling as an educative tool that doubles as a way to bond as a family and live life to the fullest.

Let's shift the paradigm together. Let's direct our energies away from competition and toward community, family, and nature. Instead of asking whether our children are "on-grade level," we can wonder: Do our children feel safe? Do our children feel loved? Satiated, both physically and mentally? Are we letting them enjoy the magic of bees?

References

Arment, A. (2019). *The call of the wild and free*. HarperOne.

Borba, M. (2021). *Thrivers: The surprising reason why some kids struggle and others shine*. Putnam.

Gray, P. (2013). *Free to learn*. Basic Books.

Heying, H., & Weinstein, B. (2021). *A hunter-gatherer's guide to the 21st century: Evolution and the challenges of modern life*. Portfolio Penguin.

McShane, M. (2021). *Hybrid homeschooling: A guide to the future of education*. Rowman & Littlefield.

National Home Education Research Institute (NHERI). (2021). Research facts on homeschooling. Retrieved July 25, 2021, from https://www.nheri.org/research-facts-on-homeschooling/

Prensky, M. (2014). *VUCA*. Retrieved July 25, 2021, from https://marcprensky.com/wp-content/uploads/2013/04/Prensky-VUCA-EDTEC-Mar-Apr-2014-FINAL.pdf

Sowder, N. (2018). *Wilder child*. Retrieved July 25, 2021, from https://wilderchild.com/about/

List of Abbreviations

AAP   American Academy of Pediatrics
ADHD   Attention Deficit / Hyperactivity Disorder
APD   Auditory Processing Disorder
ATV   All-terrain Vehicle
CAFO   Concentrated Animal Feeding Operations
DMZ   Demilitarized Zone
IGCSE   International General Certificate of Secondary Education
IGI   International General Insurance (Co.)
JAMA   Journal of the American medical Association
MBTI   Myers Briggs Type Indicator
NBL   Nature-based Learning
PISA   Program for International Student Assessment
RV   Recreational Vehicles
STEM   Science, Technology, Engineering, and Math
VPN   Virtual Private Network

1

From Structured to Stepping Back

Ginny Yurich

My plan was to be a check-the-box type of homeschool mom and being a formal public school teacher, I knew where to find the boxes. In fact, I spent an entire school year in an administrative role helping design standardized materials to be used across our school district based off of the grade level content expectations which was a fancy name for boxes that needed to be checked.

We always knew we were going to be a homeschool family. In my last year of teaching high school math, full-day kindergarten swept through our district as it did many other districts across the nation that year. While the kindergarten teachers begged to use the extra time for play and for naps, in the end it unfortunately wasn't the teachers who had the authority to make the final choice. The extra half day got slotted for academics.

Where we lived, the school bus faithfully arrived at 8:05 every morning not to return until 4:45 in the afternoon, mirroring a full eight-hour workday with commute. We had no other reason to homeschool in our early days but time. This simply felt like too much time away, and too much of the "good" time of the day. We'd heard all sorts of stories of little ones who returned home from school exhausted and cranky after navigating through a full day of teacher-directed activities, standing in lines, and weaving through complex social settings without much time set aside for decompressing.

DOI: 10.4324/9781003267362-1

Our Path to Kindergarten

It was with excited anticipation that I awaited that first year of kindergarten. My plan was to print out the grade level content expectations in our state. I even had this secret dream that I would get the checkboxes blown up at a local office store, tape them to my wall, and spend the year making sure our son would "Be enthusiastic about writing and learning to write" (W.AT.00.01) as one example. I was poised and ready for him to "Create a timeline using events from their own lives – e.g., birth, crawling, walking, loss of first tooth, first day of school" (K-H2.0.2). Certainly we would not leave off "Throws underhand with opposite foot forward" (S1.13.K) or "Drops a ball and catches it before it bounces twice" (S1.16.Ka). Pen in hand, I was ready to check the boxes, wipe my hands clean of the kindergarten year, and move on to the first grade level content expectations.

What unfolded in the years to come, would've shocked my former self. As life circumstances drew us away from a check-the-box type of school mentality, we gradually experienced more and more of an unschool life—that is, a life led by the individual interests and learning needs of our children. What has emerged is whole children filled with vibrancy, joy, passion, and learning that goes far above and beyond the boxes. Here is our story.

It was the spring before the highly anticipated kindergarten year. Though I didn't have a large swath of friends who were also homeschooling, we had a few and I realized that spring was the time to plan. Spring held homeschool conference opportunities and curriculum companies offered discounts like free shipping. The time had come to print off the content expectations, have them made into a poster, and determine how to weave all of the learning objectives into our son's first year of official schooling.

But we'd also just had a baby. She was our fourth baby, actually, and since our oldest was just entering kindergarten that meant we would have a kindergartner, a preschooler, a toddler, and an infant that first school year. Additionally, my husband lost his job and for three months was out searching for work. A move to another state was on the horizon. Finally, unrelated to the job loss, we also lost our home as the woman we were renting from was taking our rent check but not paying the mortgage. In the midst of a chaotic season, I slowly came to the realization that this was not the year for checking boxes.

Against everything I ever dreamed of, I did an about face and began to search for other options. I had a few other philosophies floating around in my mind. Our midwife sent her kids to a Waldorf school and through her I knew that the Waldorf schools didn't start reading instruction until around age seven. In fact, they used different biological markers to help determine reading readiness such as the presence of adult teeth or being able to reach up and over your head and touch your ear. I hope you just tried to do it. What these things show is that the internal organs like the eyes and the ears are fully formed, making the process of learning to read and to write that much easier.

Better Late than Early?

I had the awareness that in Finland reading instruction occurred later than it does in the states and that, somewhat counterintuitively, the reading scores in Finland were higher (Ahonen, 2020). Our journey led us down a path toward books with titles such as, *Better Late than Early* (Moore and Moore, 1989), *Learning All the Time: How Small Children Learn to Read, Write, Count, and Investigate the World Without Being Taught* (John Holt, 1990) and *Free to Learn: Why Unleashing the Instinct to Learn will Make Our Children Happier, More Self-Reliant, and Better Students for Life* (Peter Gray, 2013). These books are phenomenal resources, rich with wisdom about the ways in which children develop.

Magda Gerber (2012), an advocate for children, wrote

> Childhood is not a race to see how quickly a child can read, write and count. It is a small window of time to learn and develop at the pace that is right for each individual child. Earlier is not better.

Linda McGurk (2017), author of *There's No Such Thing as Bad Weather* wrote, "In Finland, formal teaching of reading doesn't start until the child begins first grade, at age seven… Despite this lack of emphasis on early literacy, Finland is considered the most literate country in the world" (p. 80). Fortunately, we had already bucked the system a bit by skipping preschool and I gained a certain level of confidence with that decision, knowing that it hadn't stunted or disadvantaged our kids in any way. In fact, everything was showing that our approach to the early childhood years was helping our kids develop in every facet of their being. At the charge of British educational reformer Charlotte Mason (see her work transcribed in *Home Education* published in 2017 by Living Book Press), we had spent the preschool years with a goal of spending four to six hour outdoors whenever the weather was tolerable. Life was filled with nature play, read-alouds, time in the kitchen, and snuggles on the couch. Swing sets replaced seat work and every bit of research I could get my hands on backed this approach of reserving early childhood for play and hands-on learning.

With these things in mind, as our world was in turmoil, we took a deep breath and kept our play-based approach for kindergarten. Even though life settled in a bit, we continued on in this unconventional way for first grade as well. And though my insides were in knots I could see that our kids were growing and learning things, albeit not necessarily the things that had checkboxes next to them.

My experiences henceforth mirror those of so many others. I have spent the last decade marveling at what children learn on their own, without any direction at all. In fact, with each year I am learning to continually step back even more. I no longer interrupt children who are deep in play to join me for a math lesson. Our curriculum-focused work revolves around life learning and not the other way around.

Kids Learn for Mastery

When our youngest was four she wrote her name for the first time without any instruction or prompting. We were in the midst of the hustle and bustle of getting ready for a birthday party.

Her older sister was about to turn ten and part of the birthday festivities included a spinning wheel, similar to what you'd see at a carnival, where each portion of the wheel had a prize element. The birthday girl was creating name strips for each party guest that would be pulled out a hat, signifying it was their turn to spin the wheel. Through this simple act of living life, our four-year-old grabbed a strip and proceeded to write her entire name, letter by letter, even though we had never formally shown her how to do this. Then, she asked for another strip and wrote her name again. And then she wrote it again. Over and over, we cut her strips of paper, eventually she cut her own strips of paper, and she continued on in her self-pursuit.

It has been small slivers of time, seemingly inconsequential moments just like this, that have given me the confidence to trust children. Pressed on by their own internal motivations, they learn for mastery. Our daughter could've learned to write her name in a classroom setting at the behest of a sweet teacher. But instead, she learned in context. She wanted her name in that hat. And once she wrote it the first time, it was her own excitement and her own feedback loops that drove her on. In fact, this simple act led to other fine-motor work as she took over cutting the strips of paper.

It was scary to embrace the unknown. To wait when we could've barreled forward with lesson plans felt irresponsible at times, even with an arsenal of research backing this learning approach. But the payoff was huge. To have a front-row seat where we were able to watch our children unfold on their own timelines and in their own ways has been nothing short of awe-inspiring. Additionally, since kids learn for mastery, the curriculum that they determined for themselves was far superior to any plan we could've come up with for them.

1000 Hours Outside™

These days I advocate for childhoods that are filled with open-ended nature play experiences through a movement I started called "1000 Hours Outside™." 1000 Hours Outside™ is a mission to infuse 1000 hours of time outside into a 365-day period. Families join in on the journey any time, though many like to start at the beginning of a calendar year as a New Year's Resolution. On our website, www.1000hoursoutside.com, we offer free printables that contain 1000 squares or shapes to color in throughout the year, each space representing an hour of outdoor experiences. This simple concept ensures a year that is chock full of those kinds of moments that fill our life to the brim while simultaneously laying a firm foundation for learning for years to come. Many who have embarked on this journey have messaged about moments they would've missed, if not for being intentional to weave time in the open air into their days and weeks.

The 1000 Hours Outside™ tracker charts are a way to model balance in a world where screens are designed to have a strong pull. In our family, we are learning to fill life with what we want to fill it with first and give the leftover time to screen use—not the other way around. All around the globe, families report that kids love filling out their charts and in an ironic twist of events, families are taking their charts, blowing them up at the local office store, and putting them up on their walls to fill in throughout the year. In the end, we found ourselves with very different types of checkboxes. Whereas I thought I wanted checkboxes derived from the government, we've ended up with checkboxes that give the gift of time to children.

What the child finds worthy to pursue is a worthy pursuit. It is counterintuitive to trust what a small child brings to the table, but the more we do it the easier it becomes. That first year of life is filled with moments of wonder. The first "coo," the first smile, the first roll, the first step. These milestones are fascinating every time. The remainder of childhood can continue to be this awe-inspiring if we would only continue to step back, watch, and cheer—just like how we did when they were babies.

A Return to Balance

According to Coyle (2017), a writer for the National Wildlife Refuge, the average American child spends four to seven hours of time on screened devices daily but only four to seven minutes in open-ended daily nature play. We are not an anti-screen family as our children are growing up in a technological age. We are, however, striving for balance in a day and age when it is desperately needed. Pediatric occupational therapist Angela Hanscom (2016), author of *Balanced and Barefoot* and founder of the Timbernook program, reported that children should be outside daily for uninterrupted play for at least two or three hours. Her charge doesn't stop when kids are young. Even teens should be playing outside.

Our switch from a programs-oriented, adult-directed childhood led our family from a place where we were struggling and drowning to a place where we were all thriving, and the switch happened overnight. One four-hour day at a local park at the prompting of the works of Charlotte Mason, gave us a day where we could breathe, relax, and enjoy each other and our world. This day was the start of 1000 Hours Outside™ though we didn't know it at the time.

In the years to come, I would begin to learn how what seems like a frivolous use of time is actually a learning environment, complete with opportunities to enhance cognitive and physical abilities as well as social skills. My learning continues to this day. Just as we continue to discover additional reasons to home educate, we also continue to uncover reasons to be in nature.

✅ Do Something

- ◆ Take a period of time to step back. Observe what your child learns without prompting and without interference. Marvel at it. Write it down. Create a journal. These experiences will give you confidence to continue on a path of child-led learning.
- ◆ Join in on the 1000 Hours Outside™ movement. Kids need time. They've always needed time. Open-ended time allows children to learn who they are, explore their surroundings, figure out how to enjoy their own company, and learn how to structure their free time. Not only will

you have fun and add lifetime memories to your years, but you will also be modeling balance, while at the same time providing unparalleled learning opportunities to childhood.

♦ Read some biographies. What you'll find is that life is a journey for most and that life success is rarely traced back to seat work or time spent in a classroom. Rather, it is the experiences, the failures, the relationships, and moments that are actually lived that lead to the types of lives we want to read about.

♦ Add open-ended toys to your home, ones that emulate the abundance in nature, for the times when you can't get outdoors to play. Natural elements pair beautifully with play dough. You can add scents and textures to your dough with things like wildflowers or herbs. Wooden toys and blocks aid in imaginative play as children create worlds out of the simplest of means.

♦ Share your experiences. When your child learns something that you didn't explicitly teach, tell others! Through the stories of friends and family and others in our circle of influence, we all gain confidence to parent and to educate in ways that although are tried and true, are also scary because they are counterculture.

References

Ahonen, A.K. (2020). Finland: Success through equity—the trajectories in PISA performance. In Crato, N. (Ed.) *Improving a country's education.* Springer.

Coyle, K.J. (2017). *Digital technology's role in connecting children and adults to nature and the outdoors.* Retrieved October 18, 2021, from https://www.nwf.org/~/media/PDFs/Kids-and-Nature/NWF_Role-of-Technology-in-Connecting-Kids-to-Nature_6-30_lsh.ashx

Gerber, M. (2012). *Your self-confident baby: How to encourage your child's natural abilities—from the very start.* Wiley.

Gray, P. (2013). *Free to learn: Why unleashing the instinct to learn will make our children happier, more self-reliant, and better students for life.* Basic Books.

Hanscom, A. (2016). *Balanced and barefoot: How unrestricted outdoor play makes for strong, confident, and capable children*. New Harbinger Publications.

Holt, J. (1990). *Learning all the time: How small children learn to read, write, count, and investigate the world without being taught*. Da Capo Books.

Mason, C.M. (2017). *Home education*. Living Book Press.

McGurk, L. (2017). *There's no such thing as bad weather: A Scandinavian mom's secret for raising healthy, resilient, and confident kids*. Touchstone.

Moore, R., & Moore, D. (1989). *Better late than early: A new approach to young children's education*. Reader's Digest Association.

2

The Greenhouse Effect

Joel Salatin

My wife Teresa and I had just had our first child six weeks ago, a son born 2 June 1981. We were on our first excursion outside the farm with the new baby. In our $50 1965 Dodge Coronet we headed out the driveway to the annual meeting of the Virginia Association of Biological Farmers at the president's farm located about an hour away.

Both of us had attended public schools and private Christian colleges, where we became steeped in the vision of private schooling. We embraced it completely, but as newlyweds squeaking by on one salary and trying to launch a farm endeavor we had a problem: money. We were committed to a non-public option, but no private school in our area, religious or otherwise, was within our budget.

This conundrum nagged at us but fortunately we had a couple of years before crossing that bridge so we hoped something would solve our dilemma. As we turned out of the driveway I realized *Focus on the Family* (Daly & Fuller, 2021) was on the radio, so I reached over and flicked it on. Do you know how turning the radio on catches people in mid-sentence?

I turned it on and heard the word "homeschool." I remember like yesterday not even taking my hand off the radio knob, looking at Teresa, and saying: "I have no idea what that is, but

DOI: 10.4324/9781003267362-2

that's what we're doing." Wonderful wife that she was (and is) she smiled agreeably and we listened to an interview with early homeschooling gurus Raymond and Dorothy Moore. They created the homeschool movement in the conservative community, with their foundational books *Homegrown Kids* (Moore & Moore, 1984) and *Better Late than Early* (Moore & Moore, 1989).

As soon as we returned from the farm shindig, I purchased all the Moore books and devoured them. Shortly after that I found John Holt and his newsletter *Growing Without Schooling*[1] and his term, "unschooling." I read everything I could about unorthodox education and realized that the most important thing is simply to incorporate children into adult life.

That seemed axiomatic to me, but as I looked around, I realized how foreign such a concept was in our segregated culture. Children spent far more time at the institutional school, interacting with other children and teachers, than they did actually interacting with parents in the real world. As an ecological farmer who detests Concentrated Animal Feeding Operations (CAFOs), I decided to call modern conventional institutional school "CAFOs for kids."

Sometimes people in the system find a way to break free, like New York Teacher of the Year John Taylor Gatto, whose *Dumbing Us Down* (2017) analyzed the fallacies of rigid institutional instruction. His points are timelessly prescient, like questioning why students should interrupt their curiosity at the sound of a bell, or why the only things worth learning are what the teacher says are important. These are salient broadsides against a ferociously bureaucratic system.

As we read that early literature from the 1970s and 1980s, we became increasingly committed to simply incorporating the children into our adult lives in all its aspects. We never hired a babysitter. Ours were the only children at our ten-year college reunion—and everyone loved them because they were well behaved and enjoyable to be around. We never bought toys— they played with Tupperware inventoried in the kitchen cabinets. All those shapes and colors provided untold hours of discovery.

We used cloth diapers. We never had a stroller. We never bought a jar of baby food—ever. We never had a bottle—ever. Teresa nursed and then we used our little handy dandy food mill tucked easily into the diaper bag. The children ate whatever we ate; we just ground it for them. We never had a television, and still don't. As the children got older, they learned to enjoy classic radio drama for entertainment. Does it get any better than Abbot and Costello?

We read. My, did we read. Hours and hours we'd read all the classics like *Swiss Family Robinson* (Wyss, 1812) that Teresa and I hadn't read in school. We didn't have time because we were doing busy work to keep us occupied while somebody else got the teacher's attention. As we read more about homeschooling, we learned that the average child only gets a few minutes a week of direct adult-child interaction, which is the catalyst to learning and developing curiosity.

Our modern family and vocational protocols segregate the family more than historically normal cultures. Kids go to school. Dad and Mom go to their separate jobs. Come home late in the day, eat supper, go to bed, repeat. This creates outside-of-home stimulation that hampers generational value transfer. As I researched alternative schooling in those early days, the theme that surfaced in both the conservative (Moore) and liberal (Holt) camps was generational values transfer.

Neither group pulled their children out of public schools for a better education. The driving goal was to ensure generational values transfer by reducing both peer dependency and tutelage under oppositional worldviews. Offensive behavior and instruction spanned politics, religion, recreation, morality, ethics, and even vocations. To help illustrate this point, I used my farming context to develop the idea of greenhouse kids.

Greenhouses protect tender seedlings until they can thrive in harsher outdoor environments. The goal of a greenhouse is not to keep the plant inside, but to get it strong enough to thrive outside. Likewise, the goal of spending more time with our kids was not to cloister them from buffeting values, but to shelter them long enough to adopt our values. Just like plants must be hardened off before being transplanted outside, exposing our children to opposing values within the protection of the family keeps them from being emotionally, spiritually, or physically shredded by "unfriendlies."

Fortunately, with both Teresa and I working on the farm, we had a conducive environment to integrate every minute of the day with our children. The old adage "more is caught than taught" speaks directly to the lie that time isn't important as long as it's quality time. No, it's just time.

When our son Daniel was still in diapers, I'd take him out with me to work and one spring I had to replace a boundary fence with a neighbor. I'd pace myself by taking a drink of water only after every third post. Daniel had his Tonka toys playing in the dirt I'd dig out of the post holes and as children are wont to do would begin whining for a drink of water. "Not until I finish that next post," I'd reply.

He grew up that way and eventually got big enough to help shovel the dirt and tamp in the posts on other fence projects. A family moved in nearby with a son about his age and we became friends. The boys were about 9 years old and decided to build a fort together. The moms decided on the play date and Teresa took our son over to the neighbor's place to build the fort. About an hour later the phone rang and it was the neighbor mom: "What's with your son? He won't let mine have a drink of water until they finish the first wall!"

Did I say more is caught than taught? He's still a workaholic, just like me. Our daughter had several girl friends when she was about that same age and they decided to publish a little newsletter called the Ladybug. When Thanksgiving rolled around, all the girls wrote articles about what they were thankful for and our daughter's was titled "Thankful for Work." Her thesis was that if it weren't for work, the world would be ugly and not nearly as enjoyable a place to live. Yes, more is caught than taught.

I'm a big believer in child entrepreneurship. I had my first chicken business at 10 years old and it was foundational for my identity today. Our son began a rabbit business when he was eight and is now a rabbit guru in the agricultural community. Our daughter began baking zucchini bread and selling it at about the same age. We don't believe in allowances—nobody should get paid for breathing. Both made their own money with their businesses and received affirmation from happy customers. That beats being the top scorer on a video game any time of day.

Today, our grandchildren all have personal entrepreneurial enterprises: ducks, sheep, and exotic chickens. The sweet spot for child businesses is 8–10 years of age. Prior to eight years they don't really grasp money, balance sheets, profit, and loss. After 10, they often become peer-aware and lose that child-like intrepid spirit: "I have pretty chicks; would you like to buy some?"

My granddaughter was about 5 years old when she went out and picked a handful of wildflowers from the pasture. She walked up to a customer in the farm store, a young fellow about 30, and holding the flowers aloft, said "I picked these flowers and I'm sure your wife would enjoy them; I'm selling them for a dollar." Without pausing for a response, she had plan B ready: "And if you don't have a wife, I'm sure you know a lady who would love a bouquet of flowers." Folks, 13-year-olds don't do that. By that time they are far too self-conscious. Start 'em early.

Another idea that stood out to me in those early days of getting acquainted with the reasons for homeschooling was the notion of "disassociated learning." When thinking back on my own public school institutional experiences, I don't know how many times I would groan "why do we have to learn this?" It was a common refrain and indicated a lack of association, or real-life need, on the part of the student for the information being presented.

Our son was a late reader and it created quite a tension in our extended family, which was full of schoolteachers. When he turned 10 years old, his 4-H club elected him to an office and on the way that night after the meeting he made a grand announcement: "Well, I guess if I'm going to be secretary I'm going to have to learn how to read." Within the next month, he began reading on his own and within two months was reading just about anything you could put in front of him. That illustrates associated learning, which is the opposite of disassociated learning.

When you perceive a need to know, somehow you figure out how to learn the material … fast. For some strange reason, though, parents don't trust their children to be inquisitive enough and competitive enough to learn things they decide would be beneficial for success and development. Our daughter began reading extremely early. They both had the same home routine but took an interest in different things.

Our son devoured outdoor survival skill information and loved the farm like I did. Before he could read he could drive the tractor, move a herd of cows, build deadfall traps, hunt, fish, and take visitors on tours of the farm. Unfortunately, none of that is on a standardized test; all that knowledge is meaningless in a conventional sterile academic setting. Even though he never received a high school diploma, today he manages day-to-day operations on a farm with a staff of 20 people.

Our daughter finished high school requirements at 16 and by 20 years old had two secondary associate degrees. Both children had $20,000 in the bank from their entrepreneurial business earnings. Clearly, they learned the value of a dollar, hard work, how to creatively solve production problems, and how to serve customers. None of that is on a standardized achievement test.

At 15 years old our daughter ran a house cleaning business and employed others as part-time help. She ran the operation before she could even drive herself to her clients. But none of that character and skill is measured on an aptitude test.

The single most important factor in education is curiosity. How do you stimulate curiosity? Normally it comes from living life. When we disallow children to live real life, we stifle their curiosity. Seeking new information about something springs from wrestling with real day-to-day problems. While I'm not a fan of abusing children, I do believe that our over-burdensome child labor laws preclude the kind of real-life issues that stimulate curiosity. Goodness, children scarcely even have chores anymore. Throughout most of human history children helped plant, weed, harvest, butcher, cut firewood, milk the cow, churn butter, mend clothes, cook from scratch, and a host of other foundational living skills. Participating in these life necessities informs who we are, develops our personal identity, and uncovers our passions.

Our son routinely said "I can do any math problem if you put it in dollars and cents." Why? Because he had to maintain his rabbit financial records, run margins, percentages, and all the other requirements of running a business. Percentages are just some esoteric unnecessary idea until you figure margins, mortality rates, and a host of other mathematical computations necessary to running a business.

One of the reasons we have a crisis of identity among our young people today is because they are generally denied the opportunity to integrate continuously and intimately with the adult world. They're plopped in front of the television, handed a video game, or hovered over and disempowered from decision-making for their own destiny. Their decisions are limited to someone else' idea of what is important. But if we want responsible decision-making, we must exercise it, like a muscle. Discernment is a muscle and it doesn't suddenly pop into existence at 20 years old.

Decisional consequences, both success and failure, enable a young person to exercise discernment, which imparts wisdom. One of the most interesting school models I've ever encountered was in New Mexico at Camino de Paz, a farm school for ages 12–15 year-olds. At this school, the farm did not augment the curriculum; the farm was the curriculum. Everything on the academic side emanated from the students' farm work.

They raised, butchered, packed, and sold pastured chickens. They milked goats and made cheese. Monitoring bacteria counts through a microscope created intense interest in the world of microbes. They had greenhouses and gardens, offering agronomy, entomology, and math problems to solve. If you're going to plant beets on 3-inch centers in rows a foot apart, how many beets will you have per square yard of garden space?

Believe me, when children are this connected to their education, you can't throttle back their curiosity. They want to know about the bugs they see, the worms in the soil, the reasons this tomato is healthy and that one isn't. The real world offers unlimited problems and interesting conditions to solve. While an elementary classroom with some plants and two chicks can try to bring some of this ecological umbilical into the institutional setting, it's all fabricated, fantasy, unreal. Out in the garden, in the field, in real world production it's not just interesting; information is survival. Knowing things is the difference between the whole enterprise succeeding or failing. It isn't just the teacher's project. These middle schoolers not only produced their own food, butchered, and processed it, they cooked their own meals, preserved their food, and sold the excess at the local farmers' market.

They sheared a handful of sheep, cleaned, carded, and spun the wool and handcrafted cell phone purses and other accessories. Interacting with customers at the market, selling their wares, keeping track of their money, learning the background of the animal and plant genetics—all of these things imbued these young people with intense personal ownership in their education. When I visited the school to do a fundraiser, every one of these youngsters greeted me with direct eye contact, shook my hand with firmness and confidence, and hustled me out to the fields to show me their farming endeavors.

The only thing I could think when I left there was how tragic it is that all youngsters don't have the same opportunity. Using real-life experience and participation to contextualize a curriculum fundamentally de-institutionalizes the instructional model. Need drives curiosity; curiosity drives learning.

Most parents don't have enough faith in their own children to believe that youngsters will learn what they need to when they see the need to. Rather than cramming our information down their throat in a sterile setting, how about incorporating our kids into our adult lives to such an extent that they become miniature adults?

This brings me to the question of socialization. Our home-school mentors, Rick and Marilyn Boyer, who had a dozen children and are gurus in the conservative brand of parent-driven schooling, make a strong distinction between being socialized and being sociable. Most adults say the word socialized when what they really mean is sociable. The difference is profound.

Socialization means doing what everyone else does. Its etymological closeness to socialism and socialist indicates its thematic thread toward homogenization. The word sociable, however, delineates social graces, like being kind, polite, and diplomatic.

The more our children are around peers, the more socialized they become. The more they are around adults, the more sociable they become. Why? Children, especially when young, say "me" constantly. "Mine, mine, mine" they demand, standing with a fist-clenched toy. By the time humans become adults, hopefully they've learned about service, mercy, gentleness, gratitude and other graces beyond "me." That's what being sociable is all about.

Since Teresa and I were starting out as poor farmers and we began home schooling before it became a household word, we simply purchased used schoolbooks from the public school discard sales. We discovered a most interesting thing. The math books were half review from the previous year. As a result, with both of our children when they started the next grade level of math, we'd let them take the chapter tests until they were unable to answer.

Each time, they went halfway through the book. That's where we started and we realized in a regular classroom, half the school year was simply a review of the previous year. From a sheer efficiency standpoint, this customized acceleration saved hours and hours of tedium that would have been spent daydreaming, throwing spitballs, and otherwise getting into trouble—being socialized.

Perhaps the most powerful unorthodox teaching tip I learned during those early years of research: you're not doing this to school at home. Many parents obsess over rigid curricula, even doing bulletin boards and recess periods. This protocol essentially transports the institutional model to the home. It irritates the children and burns out the parents.

The whole beauty of unschooling, homeschooling, or whatever name you want to call wildly de-institutionalized education is that it can be spontaneous, practical, and directed by self-interest. If a child is suddenly interested in fabrics, you can study clothing throughout history, which leads to the people, which leads to history, which leads to politics, religion, economics, and philosophy. If we let the natural inquisitiveness drive learning, it's far more efficient and enjoyable.

COVID-19 has brought the term "pod schools" to the educational lexicon. Parents desperate to see their children continue learning got together and hired a teacher. While this may not go far enough into the creative as some of us would like, it's a wonderful step away from the institutional setting. Scale does matter. It matters in farming, in kitchens, and in social groups.

A setting with 5–10 children is completely different to a setting with 300, no matter the administration, building, or quality of teachers. Scale in and of itself changes everything. In most of our American jurisdictions, per pupil allocations average a little over $12,000 per year (Education Data, 2021). Especially in lower grades, most teachers are women, and many of them have young children. Imagine if the school district were to encourage any credentialed teacher to choose to leave the institutional classroom and stay home to host a pod school.

Thousands and thousands of teachers using day care could stay home with their own children and teach 5–10 others for half a day, earn their normal salary without having to own a second car, drive to work, and answer to top-heavy administrative bureaucrats. At least in the formative years, students would enjoy an extremely low teacher-student ratio and the pod schools would be embedded in neighborhoods where parents could feel wanted and involved.

One of the most telling conversations I ever had with our county's public school superintendent occurred at a public hearing regarding raising taxes to give more money to the school division. I testified that I had teachers who should have been fired years before I had them, and I had others who should have received twice the salary they were paid, but nobody asked me. In fact, nobody ever asks. I told the supervisors that unless and until someone asks me which teachers were good and which were bad I was opposed to any additional taxes going to the schools.

The superintendent accosted me in the hallway outside the public hearing room and said, "You have no right to testify here; your kids aren't in the public school." This is the typical arrogance of the conventional school establishment. Never mind that I was a taxpayer, voter, and was paying for my own children's education economically and emotionally. I believe this attitude is common in the orthodox educational establishment.

The best way to check this arrogance and bureaucratic elitism is to pursue the road less traveled, and march to the beat of a different drummer. Indeed the professional and instructional help to enable folks to own their educational experience has never been more readily available, cheaper, and eclectic. It is time to bring choice to our children and their educational experience. It is time for parents to be mentors. It is time for education to be effective. The next generation deserves nothing less.

✅ Do Something

- ◆ Grow something, whether in a pot or, if you have room, in the ground, and make it family project.
- ◆ Brainstorm something you wish existed in your community and see if your child could offer that service or product as an entrepreneur.
- ◆ Cook from scratch and let your children do ingredient measurements and figure the fractions.
- ◆ Get 2–5 chickens to eat your kitchen scraps and give you eggs; it's as close to magic as anything you'll ever see. My book *Polyface Micro* tells you how to do this even in an apartment.
- ◆ Get rid of the television.
- ◆ Eliminate video games from your family's life.
- ◆ With the extra time, plan one excursion a month to visit a local farm and begin patronizing integrity food.
- ◆ Sign your kids up for a farm camp.
- ◆ Put in a garden and record how much you can cut your grocery bill.
- ◆ Install a simple solarium on the side of your house to extend your growing season.

Note

1 Holt's newsletters have been published in various forms. See: Holt, J. (1997). *Growing without schooling: A record of a grassroots movement*, Vol 1: August 1977–December 1979.

References

Daly, J., & Fuller, J. (2021). *Focus on the family*. Retrieved September 27, 2021, from https://www.focusonthefamily.com/shows/broadcast/

Gatto, J.T. (2017). *Dumbing us down*. New Society Publishers.

Moore, R., & Moore, D. (1984). *Homegrown kids*. W Pub Group.

Moore, R., & Moore, D. (1989). *Better late than early: A new approach to young children's education*. Reader's Digest Association.

Wyss, J.D. (1812). *Swiss family Robinson*. JD Wyss.

3

A Unique Education

Unschooling to Adulthood

Ben Riley & Gina Riley

When I was born, my mom (Dr. Gina Riley) was a young single mother with limited financial resources but ample confidence and determination to be the best mother she could possibly be. She noticed that I was a very curious, intrinsically motivated, and natural learner who was also somewhat shy and introverted. By the time I was five years old, I began to become obsessed with rocks, had memorized most of the periodic table of elements, and had developed a keen interest in the world around me through reading and frequent trips to museums, libraries, and community centers. For me, the distinction between life and learning was nonexistent. Learning was not viewed as a chore or something to do only during school hours; instead, it was simply a natural part of life. As a result, my mom did not see the need to send me to school, as I was already well above my grade level in most subjects. She also knew that my being an attached, curious, and quiet kid would not fit well in a traditional public school, and thus school would not be the ideal educational environment for me.

From an early age, my mom allowed and encouraged me to make my own decisions as much as possible. This included the

DOI: 10.4324/9781003267362-3

choice to unschool. Unschooling is a variation of homeschooling where, instead of following a set curriculum, children learn through everyday life experiences. These experiences are of their choosing and tend to match their strengths, interests, and personal learning styles (Wheatley, 2009). In unschooling, there are no assignments, no set curriculum, and no structured assessments. Within an unschooling environment, parents do not directly teach or provide direct instruction. Instead, they provide an environmental context that supports their child's learning and development (Gray & Riley, 2013).

At the end of every academic year, my mom would ask me if I wanted to continue unschooling, and if so, why. In the early years, the decision was easy: I was having lots of fun playing, exploring, and just living life. This was the first major reason I wanted to continue unschooling: we weren't "doing school." Instead, we were living life and learning all the time.

In the middle years, the decision became more complex, as outside opinions and perspectives became more influential. Family members, neighbors, friends, and people from the local community would continually question (sometimes very harshly) the validity of homeschooling, say that I was "missing out," or state that they thought homeschooling was not as good as "real" school. They would even sometimes test me on school subjects, slipping math problems into casual conversations. Luckily, I was an intelligent and well-read kid, so they were likely disappointed that I did so well on their tests! However, that constant outside perspective influenced me and led me to briefly question my own education during my early adolescent years. I would seriously wonder if I was actually missing out on something important by not going to public school. This came to a head at age 12, when I expressed a vague interest in going to school. My mom researched several local schools over the summer and asked me to do the same. I wish I could say that I carefully and thoroughly researched all my options and came to a well-informed decision. The truth was less glamorous: I did not research any schools and said that I wanted to continue unschooling, simply because it was the option that took the least effort for me at that point. As a result, we continued unschooling.

Gina's Perspective

The criticism was not fun, but not surprising either. In 2013, Dr. Peter Gray and I did a qualitative study of 232 families who chose to unschool. When asked about the challenges of unschooling, the most frequent challenge, noted by 43.5 percent of participants, was identified as social pressure or criticism regarding the choice to unschool by relatives, neighbors, and friends. These families reported negative judgments from almost everyone regarding their decision to unschool. As one parent expressed, "The biggest hurdle has been other people. It's difficult to find others who are encouraging, especially people who live nearby" (Gray & Riley, 2013). Unschooling families also felt a constant need to justify their choice to others. This constant negative judgment and criticism was perceived as exhausting and anxiety provoking (Gray & Riley, 2013). In Rolstad and Kesson's (2013) study of self-efficacy in unschooling mothers, many expressed how debilitating this incessant criticism can be. It is especially difficult when criticism comes from inside the family. As one unschooling parent shared within the Gray and Riley (2013) study, "We still have not told my husband's family that we are unschooling. We fear they would panic and feel the need to step in. We don't want that tension for ourselves or our children." Another parent shared, "My parents are both public school teachers who don't understand our decision to unschool. They barrage our children constantly with curriculum-based questions. We regularly have conversations about the choice and their disagreement with it." Even when they were not receiving or responding to public or verbal criticism, unschooling parents ceaselessly seem to work through imagined dialogue with critics (O'Hare & Coyne, 2020), both internally and through blog or social media postings.

This internal and external dialogue can be annoying at best, deeply hurtful at its worst. When we were unschooling I remember numerous conversations I had with family and friends who would incessantly ask, "when are you planning on sending your child to school?" As my son grew older and heard more of those critiques, I realized it was time for me to set boundaries.

On a personal note, I feel some cognitive dissonance regarding my position on both public schooling and unschooling. Although my research life revolves around unschooling and self-directed learning, and I personally have unschooled my own child, I spend a majority of my time every day working to make public education better. I am a professor of teacher education and coordinate a program that certifies adolescent special educators to teach in the largest school system in the United States. I believe deeply in my teacher candidates and their power to change public schools for the better. I see how much they care for their students, and how much time they devote to making their students' lives better. I love and respect each and every one of my teacher candidates, and genuinely honor their work. When I visit public schools, I see first-hand the dedication administrators, teachers, and staff have with regard to their schools and the students they serve. I live my life shuffling between two worlds, seeing the pros and cons of each. It gives me great perspective, but it is still sometimes taxing. Most of those who support unschooling are not against public schools, teachers, or formal systems of learning. Instead, we see the benefits of self-directed, intrinsically motivated learning and want to share those benefits with the world (or just with our individual children).

The Later Years – Ben's Perspective

In the later years, the choice whether or not to continue home-schooling was easy. I had now found a specialization (music), wanted to spend most of my free time studying and playing music, and knew that this would only be possible if we continued unschooling. I was able to not only try different interests, but actually have the time and space to develop these interests however far I wanted to take them.

In Riley and Gray's study of unschooled adults (2015), 77% of participants stated that the largest advantage of unschooling was time to pursue one's own interests. As an example, one participant shared, "As a teenager, I cherished that unschooling led me to pursue my interests. It also opened up experiences that are extremely unlikely I would have had the opportunity for if I was schooled." Another wrote that "unschooling gave me the ability to process things deeply, to spend all day curled up with my journal imagining possibilities. It also gave me opportunity to become intimate with my interests" (Gray & Riley, 2015). Adult unschooler Astra Taylor (2020) remembers that "In our house, the adults encouraged our interests, even those they found inscrutable, but did not instruct us or judge our progress. I spent months obsessed with making balloon animals."

The Teen Years

Everyone loves the idea of unschooling their little ones! Years of exploration and wonder, check! Field trips to the farm, the zoo, and the playground, check! But what happens when a child becomes older? What about unschooling during the teen years?

For me (Ben), the teen years were a time of increased specialization and individuality. During this time, I learned a lot about the world around me, my place in it, and the skills needed to function and thrive in society as we know it. This included many instances of bad moods and stubbornness on my part, as well as making many significant strides forward in my life and work. For example, during my teen years, I wanted to do things *my* way, whatever that meant (cue the bad moods and stubbornness), found my passion (music, especially guitar), learned how to work, manage money, effectively navigate complex situations, and take on increased responsibilities (work, college courses, driving, more complex household chores, etc.). However, the most formative aspect of my teen years was unexpectedly finding and developing a deep passion for music, as this quickly became the central component of the remaining years of my unschooling experience.

When I was 13 years old, my mom was given a guitar by one of her students and began taking lessons at a local music school. She asked if I would like to try learning guitar, but I repeatedly refused. However, I began to occasionally watch my mom practice guitar and would ask something like "could you show me how to play that?" My mom, who only knew several basic chords, instead suggested that she sign me up for a month of guitar lessons with her guitar teacher, and I could quit at any time after that month. After a few more months, I agreed and began to take guitar lessons. Up to this point I had absolutely no interest in music, and definitely did not have what people call "musical talent." Within a few weeks of lessons, to the surprise of everyone in my family (including myself), I became obsessed with playing guitar. I would play it whenever I could, and because I did not go to school or follow a predetermined curriculum, I could often play guitar all day if I wanted to, and I wanted to! For the first time, I felt that I had found what I was meant to do. I had a fantastic teacher who showed me that playing music can be filled with joy, meaning, personal expression, and a deep sense of fulfillment, and this newfound discovery soon led to an all-consuming obsession with the guitar and its music.

By age 16, playing and learning about guitar was my main topic of study. That same year, our unschooling journey also became officially complete when I was awarded a "certificate of completion" from the local school district. I wanted to study guitar at a more advanced level, and also felt the need to obtain some sort of formal credentials. I knew that I wanted to attend a high quality program that was either close to home or online. As a result, I applied and was accepted to Berklee College of Music's online program. The admissions department at Berklee was not concerned in the least about my educational background, and the application process was very straightforward. During my time studying at Berklee, I attended courses in jazz, blues, and rock guitar, music theory, and music business. I had the privilege of taking classes taught by incredible musicians and educators and learned many invaluable lessons about guitar playing and overall musicianship. Two years later, at the age of 18, I completed Berklee's Master Guitar Certificate Program with a 3.96 GPA. My unschooling journey was officially finished, and my college journey had begun.

The College Experience

By this point, I had played in a band and was also playing local gigs as a solo guitarist and singer/songwriter. I thought that if I were to succeed in the music industry (whatever that meant), I would need additional credentials, and also felt that there was an expectation for me to get a bachelor's degree in order to prove that I could succeed in a formal learning environment despite my nontraditional educational background. I knew that I wanted to further my formal study of music and, more specifically, the guitar, but felt uncertain about which college I would like to attend. At least, that was until I went to an open house at Nyack College and met the dean of their music department. I was immediately struck by how kind everyone seemed, and was impressed by the expertise of the music faculty. After talking to the dean, a wonderful man who made me feel welcome right away, I applied and auditioned for the Bachelor of Music program. The admissions officer at first expressed much skepticism regarding my educational background, which quickly subsided when he saw my resume and a portfolio of my work. Long story short, I was accepted and attended Nyack College from 2014 to 2018. Nyack College was a great fit for me at the time. I felt welcomed by the faculty and fellow students and took a wide range of classes in music and other liberal arts, which broadened my perspective both on music and the world as a whole. Thanks to an excellent private teacher and much practice, I learned how to play classical guitar, and went from knowing a couple of early intermediate pieces to playing multi-movement concert repertoire within the span of four years. In 2018, I graduated summa cum laude from Nyack College with a Bachelor of Music in classical guitar performance, and felt that I had proved what I set out to prove.

Graduate School

After I graduated, I was not sure whether I wanted to continue my formal study of music. As a result, I chose to take a gap year, during which I performed, expanded my teaching studio, and applied to graduate schools. Since I was still undecided regarding whether I wanted to pursue a performance or non-performance based program, I applied to both types. The idea of taking a year between degrees did not fill me with fear of not "progressing" at the pace that may be typically expected, as I already knew from unschooling that life is a journey, rather than a set linear timetable.

After many months of work on applications, exams, and several memorable audition experiences, I ultimately made the choice to attend Hunter College's M.A. in Music program with a focus on music theory. I appreciated their holistic and multi-disciplinary approach to the study and analysis of music, the kindness, intelligence, and prestige of the faculty and fellow students, and the reasonable tuition costs. The interconnectedness of music with its broader contexts was also a recurring theme throughout my graduate studies at Hunter. Although my major was music theory, I also attended courses in a broad variety of musical disciplines, including musicology, ethnomusicology, orchestration, musicianship, style criticism, philosophies of musical identity, and research techniques. I graduated from Hunter College in Spring 2021 with a Master of Arts in Music Theory and believe that I have now finally proved that I could excel in higher education despite (actually, as a direct result of) being unschooled.

Careers and Entrepreneurship

I currently have a thriving teaching studio, work as faculty at Westchester Community College and Rivertown Music, a local music school, and also am a self-employed musician, writer, editor, and website designer. Unschooling taught me that you can shape your life to encompass your interests, preferences, and goals, and that is definitely a guiding principle in my life and work. Indeed, my career has essentially become a creatively evolving combination of the interests and topics that I explored while unschooling. I am able to share my love of music by performing and teaching, continuing to research and learn about topics of interest as a writer and editor, and highlighting my passions for these fields to a global community as a website designer. Many other unschoolers have also applied their talent, interests, and strengths to create their career paths. In fact, entrepreneurship is one of the career paths unschoolers frequently take (Riley & Gray, 2015).

Reflections on Unschooling, Life, and Learning

Life and learning, in our view, are the same, inextricably connected despite the imaginary boundaries between the two that are consistently and insidiously perpetuated by contemporary society. Throughout life, we are always learning and never intend to stop doing so. And there's absolutely nothing special about that. People know how to learn. We've been taught by society to distrust our independent capacities to learn, but we can instead choose to tap into our incredible potential and remember that learning is, as John Holt said, as natural as breathing (Holt, 1968). We are glad to have jointly made the decision to unschool and are reaping the rewards of our untraditional choice every day of our lives.

 Do Something

Plan for Dealing with Criticism
Be confident in your choice to do what is best for your family. When people ask "Why don't you send your child to school?" you can say "Unschooling is what works best for us" or "Every child needs something different; for my child, it is unschooling." In the same conversation, affirm the choices other families have made for their children. Many times, the choice to unschool may seem like a rejection of the decisions other parents have made for their own children. So give individuals who have made different choices the same respect you would want others to give to you.

For example, you can say: "I am so glad your child is enjoying school! It seems like that is what is best for your child."

Facilitate Freedom of Choice in the Teen Years

Unschooling seems easy when a child is little, and generally gets more complicated during the teen years. Remember that teens need trust and autonomy to thrive. Allow teens to pursue their interests and strengths and show autonomy support for the positive choices they make in their lives.

Create a Portfolio of Your Child's Unschooling Journey

Unschoolers may not have traditional academic transcripts, so find some way to document learning (Gina used a daily planner, and would jot down activities we did, what we read, and activities we talked about each day). This documentation helps later on if your teen chooses a more academic path, like college, and may also assist with state mandated paperwork or summaries of learning.

References

Gray, P., & Riley, G. (2013). The challenges and benefits of unschooling, according to 232 families who have chosen that route. *Journal of Unschooling and Alternative Learning, 7*(14). https://jual.nipissingu.ca/wp-content/uploads/sites/25/2014/06/v72141.pdf

Gray, P., & Riley, G. (2015). Grown unschoolers' evaluations of their unschooling experience: Report I on a survey of 75 unschooled adults. *Other Education, 4*(2), 8–32. https://www.othereducation.org/index.php/OE/article/view/104

Holt, J. (1968). *Learning all the time.* Hachette Books.

O'Hare, A., & Coyne, J. (2020). Unschooling and the self: A dialogical analysis of unschooling blogs in Australia and New Zealand. *Culture & Psychology, 26*(3), 484–499.

Riley, G., & Gray, P. (2015). Grown unschoolers' experiences with higher education and employment: Report II on a survey of 75 unschooled adults. *Other Education, 4*(2), 33–53. https://www.othereducation.org/index.php/OE/article/view/105

Rolstad, K., & Kesson, K. (2013). Unschooling, then and now. *Journal of Unschooling and Alternative Learning, 7*(14), 29–67.

Taylor, A. (2020). Perhaps it's time to consider unschooling. https://www.thecut.com/2020/03/unschooling-your-kids-during-coronavirus-quarantine.html

Wheatley, K.F. (2009). Unschooling: A growing oasis for development and democracy. *Encounter: Education for Meaning and Social Justice, 22*(2), 27–32.

Additional Resources

Csikszentmihalyi, M. (2008). *Flow: The psychology of optimal experience.* Harper Perennial Modern Classics.

Riley, B. (2017a). The power of story: Encouraging homeschoolers, unschoolers, and those who attend alternative schools to change the world through personal narrative. *Tipping Points.* https://www.self-directed.org/tp/power-of-story/

Riley, B. (2017b). A unique education. *Life Learning Magazine.* http://www.lifelearningmagazine.com/1706/unique-education.htm

Riley, B. (2020a). My experience as a home education graduate. In Rebecca English (Ed.), *Global perspectives on home education in the 21st century* (pp. 76–86). IGI Global.

Riley, B. (2020b). Sing, o muse: On the link between creativity and self-directed education. *The Journal of Unschooling and Alternative Learning, 14*(27), 31–47. https://jual.nipissingu.ca/wp-content/uploads/sites/25/2020/06/v14273.pdf

Riley, G. (2015). Differences in competence, autonomy, and relatedness between home educated and traditionally educated young adults. *International Social Science Review, 90*(2), 1–27. https://digitalcommons.northgeorgia.edu/cgi/viewcontent.cgi?article=1093&context=issr

Riley, G. (2018a). Unschooling: A direct application of Deci and Ryan's self determination theory and cognitive evaluation theory. *European Journal of Alternative Education Studies, 3*(1), 54–61. https://www.oapub.org/edu/index.php/ejae/article/view/1482

Riley, G. (2018b). Exploring unschoolers' experiences in learning to read: How reading happens within the self-directed learning environment. *Journal of Unschooling and Alternative Learning*, *12*(24), 1–33. https://jual.nipissingu.ca/wp-content/uploads/sites/25/2018/10/v12241.pdf

Riley, G. (2020). *Unschooling: Exploring learning beyond the classroom*. Palgrave Macmillan.

Riley, G. (2021). *The homeschooling starter guide*. Rockridge Press.

4

The Parent–Child Apprenticeship

Navigating Learning with Little to No Curriculum

Katie Rybakova Mathews

"This is what I was concerned about," the 3rd grade teacher said, handing over a student's worksheet. The prompt read: *If I could be anything in the world, I would be...* The student had meticulously drawn a picture of a seated woman with long brown hair, a square object in her hand. *My mom's phone.* Why? *So that she paid attention to me.*

***

This is not a chapter on technology—that deserves a book in and of itself—but rather on human education. We have existed as a species for about 200,000 years (King, 2012). Modern education—public education as we know it—has been around for about 200 years. This is but a blimp of time compared to our species. Much of learning prior to modern schooling occurred through play or conversation, the latter often over food and fire (Heying & Weinstein, 2021). As civilization changed, grew, and advanced, humans learned through an apprenticeship model with more specialized niches (Wagner & Dintersmith, 2015). Learning was focused on basic survival and communication within small clans where alloparenting (care provided by others

DOI: 10.4324/9781003267362-4

outside of mother and father) was normal and generally simple as everyone had similar values and goals.

As society advanced, learning shifted from holistic and survival-based to niche skillsets—these niches contributed to a growing population of people, or society. A boom in population meant the forming of socioeconomic classes. Hands-on labor became associated with lower socioeconomic classes while aristocrats had the money and power to hire tutors for their children's intellectual work—usually in the form of rhetoric (the art of persuasion) and the arts (Wagner & Dintersmith, 2015). The apprenticeship model was used in both blue-collar and white-collar worlds—youth (usually male) either became an apprentice to learn a trade or studied under the tutelage of a tutor. For instance, Socrates taught Plato, who then taught Aristotle (Britannica, 2021).

Wagner and Dintersmith (2015) chronicled the need for a standardized education which arose from Latin grammar schools—the need to transcribe and create replicas of the Holy Bible; "These grammar schools revolved around four educational principles: standardization, time efficiency, minimization of error, and intolerance of accidental—or God forbid—creative departures from the norm" (p. 24). The Prussian model of education—at the time considered particularly innovative—took the Latin grammar school model and applied it to create a compulsory education for its population for basic literacy skills—the "three R's" of reading, writing, and arithmetic. Horace Mann, the father of the modern public school in America, traveled to Europe and brought back the Prussian system of compulsory education to Massachusetts (Messerli, 1972). Although education and schooling prior to Horace Mann's model of public school existed, it was patchy—usually through a conglomerate of different options like church-run schoolhouses, boarding schools, and private tutoring (Kober, 2020). Mann's was the first to be free of charge, funded by the state, and available to all children (although at the time this commonly excluded people of color and girls) (Kober, 2020). The first compulsory education law for *modern* public education was passed in Massachusetts in 1852, although there had also been a mandated schooling law passed in 1642 in the colony of Massachusetts (Katz, 1976a).

In essence, continued social shifts to accommodate class systems, along with a growing human population, required that education shift from the apprenticeship model, which was typically one-on-one, to what Sir Ken Robinson (2010) quips as "in batches." In the modern public education model, children are grouped by age. In his book *Out of Our Minds*, Robinson (2017) wrote further on this topic, denouncing the way we group children "as if the most important thing that children have in common is their date of manufacture" (p. 46).

The goals of public compulsory schooling are complex, as well as dependent on who you ask. One of the goals of public compulsory schooling was to enhance the literacy levels of the general population. Another was to produce obedient workers that were the backbone of the blue-collar-run economy at the height of the Industrial Revolution. "Schools are intended to produce...formulaic human beings whose behavior can be predicted and controlled" (Gatto, 2017, p. 22). Katz (1976b) emphasized how the population during the 19th century believed that schooling would provide the "the lower-class child with an alternative environment and a superior set of adult models" (p. 393). Yet another goal was to help assimilate an influx of immigrants (Kober, 2020). While 21st century teachers recognize the fallacies and dangers of more sinister goals, there is no denying that these were some of the ideological foundations of initial public schools.

There is plenty of research and opinion on what the modern education system does and does not do for our youth; much of it is dark, with shades of gray. What is curious is that research has also shown the effectiveness of the *modern* apprenticeship model, despite it being one of the oldest methods of instruction in our species (Dennen & Burner, 2008; Fuller & Unwin, 2011; Wagner & Dintersmith, 2015). Some scholars point to the success of vocational and trade school programs that use the apprenticeship model in its most quintessential form—the passing down of a skill or trade from an experienced person to a novice (Fuller & Unwin, 2011). Some scholars categorize this modernized apprenticeship approach a cognitive apprenticeship, specifying that this is a model of metacognition and a verbalization of reflection acts versus *only* the study of a tangible skill (Dennen & Burner, 2008).

In other words, an apprenticeship can teach not only skills and trades but also cognitive skills and mindsets.

This approach, along with effective education at large, is built on multiple premises:

- ◆ The learner is motivated and interested in the subject material—a lackluster blacksmith student will become a lackluster (and sad) blacksmith.
- ◆ The learner uses observation, conversation, and models in conjunction with play, tinkering, and practice to gain fluency and accuracy in a skill—one does not learn to play tennis through reading a textbook on tennis, but rather after a coach models a swing and then hands over the racquet for the player to have a go at it.
- ◆ The learner receives timely and detailed feedback (in other words, assessment), then has the opportunity to revise or try again—no one-and-done worksheets. Think of the feedback an infant receives learning to walk. *Thump*—ouch. The infant is the apprentice and the environment is the tutor, if only through metaphor. The infant also does not give up trying to walk, bumps and all.
- ◆ The learner is able to break larger skills into smaller steps alongside a mentor who models and guides the process (Dennen & Burner, 2008). The task is also within the learner's zone of proximal development—a fancy term that in essence means the child will be sufficiently challenged but not too much so and would need the assistance of a mentor to successfully complete the task and thus learn. If I place a hoop in front of you and ask you to shoot a balled-up piece of paper into it, it would be too easy. Too far, and it would be too difficult. Just the right amount of challenge, with a helpful hint or two about arcing the balled-up paper, and you have learned to aim into a bin.
- ◆ The learner has an opportunity to shift their motivations and interests as they expand their knowledge of the world. If I were required to pursue my initial career aspiration as a freshman in college, I'd be a very sad genetic engineer.

◆ The learner can seek out mentees in their pursuit of knowledge and play outside of their age bracket. We have not been designed to learn in same-age batches. Children and adolescents benefit greatly from apprenticeships and mentor opportunities regardless of their age. A 3-year-old can ignite joy and curiosity in a grumpy 15-year-old (there is a reason they are called sophomores after all), much like a 5-year-old can benefit greatly from learning to share from a 7-year-old.

Through the apprenticeship model, young humans learn about the world, as well as how to react to it. I stubbed my toe on my youngest daughter's highchair, and instead of saying what I really wanted to say I exclaimed "Yowza!" only to hear my eldest toddler parrot this very phrase not ten minutes later in a mock dramatic staging of "I subbed my toe on this table." This moves well beyond a traditional education of learning Shakespearian sonnets and how to structure a five-paragraph essay. This kind of learning occurs regardless of whether students go to public or private school, homeschool, or hybrid homeschool. In essence, we, as parents, are the mentor, and our children, the apprentices.

While a traditional apprenticeship might be used to learn a specific skill or trade, or perhaps even thought process, the 21st century apprenticeship emphasizes value and life, not just skill. Education moves beyond reading, writing, and math into critical thinking skills and intangibles such as innovation and education (Robinson, 2017). Drill and kill worksheets and scripted curriculum might help teach rote memorization and basic facts, but they do not teach entrepreneurship, lifelong readership, and joy in learning. In our role as the tutor and our children's role as the apprentice, we serve as the ultimate model for soft skills and engaging with life. If we want to instill the value of joy in our children, we need to be joyful ourselves.

In a homeschooling environment, then, we get to wear a fancy hat called teacher, when in reality we've been teaching our children about the world all along—we now just have more of an opportunity to do it. This does not mean we need to be perfect, but that we do need to take a moment in thinking about education to consider how we model everyday life. For instance, I am terrible at taking breaks. I'm not a great model for that. But, every morning, my husband and I "co-teach" by observing the sky. *Wow, look at the show the sun is putting on for us this morning, with the hues of pink and purple brushstrokes.* I've got a book in every corner of our house and am reading at least two of them at any given time. I cry when I read *The Giving Tree*. Our daughters are learning to find beauty in nature, surround themselves with stories, and engage in a book with emotion and empathy (and not take breaks; but we are working on that). This is the apprenticeship model at work.

More often than not we find ways to entertain our children rather than engage them. Here, play with this pot and pan or watch TV while I make dinner. Engaging our children, of course in a developmentally appropriate way, in our daily tasks means we subconsciously communicate with them that they are part of the family team and that they are a *responsible* member of the family. The reality of it is that this might initially mean a task that could take us ten minutes ends up taking thirty, or that our gingerbread houses don't look like they do on Pinterest. In *Hunt, Gather, Parent*, Doucleff (2021) shared multiple examples of how astounding it was to see children—from teenagers to toddlers—"do chores" without being asked to. It came down to the ways in which the family members instilled the value of living together in a home; rather than using a chore chart or basic behaviorism (e.g. clean plates for two dollars), the expectation was that the child, from when they were able to, contributed and helped when parents engaged in daily chores. This often was as early as toddler-age.

Doing the dishes, cooking dinner, and tending to livestock, however, is not typically what we envision when we think of educating a child. If we ask ourselves what our children need in terms of the "fundamentals," we'll gravitate to things like knowing their times tables, basic literacy skills, and, as children get older, knowledge about concepts or events like the Holocaust or the Pythagorean theorem. Much like most traditional schools silo subjects, we gravitate to shelving educational topics into neat categories—science, math, English, social studies—when in actuality and in real life these shelves don't exist. Robinson (2017) reminded us, for instance, that we erroneously conflate academics with education, which then is tied erroneously with intellect; "if human intelligence were limited to [academic ability] most of human culture would never have happened" (Robinson, 2017, p. 52).

Education cannot be teased apart from living. We learn every day through experiences, so instead of focusing on curriculum, we focus on providing rich and deep experiences in the things we value most as a family. If we value worldliness, we travel far and wide. If we value work ethic, we might farm, play a sport, or engage in a variety of activities that we learn through *doing* versus from a textbook (and that's coming from someone who has made a career out of knowledge from books). If we value entrepreneurship, we might encourage our children to start their own business or attend an entrepreneurship conference for kids and young adults.

Can curriculum be a part of the educational process? If both you and your children are interested and motivated about a subject, topic, or experience, absolutely. We can teach fundamentals in authentic ways without forcing it.

What does a parent teach a child when they are focused more on their phone than on their child most of the time? They teach them that being digitally engaged is more important than being engaged in real life. A child that sits down to watch TV while mom or dad make dinner learns that their job, and their place, is to be entertained while food is being prepared. A child forced to memorize and then regurgitate Shakespearian verse learns, at best, to do what he is told, and at worst, to hate Shakespeare and anything to do with memorization.

Homeschooling, then, is a tremendous responsibility on us as parents. We have the luxury of more time with our children. What a wondrous thing. It also means more opportunity for both implicit and explicit apprenticeships. It is our jobs, then, to act less as what our minds conjure up as "teachers" and more like curators, astute observers, and coaches.

This is not an original thought. Montessori (1986), for instance, has underscored the necessity for teachers to observe children as keenly as scientists studying the natural world. She also elaborated that "The strength of even the smallest children is more than we imagine, but it must have free play in order to reveal itself" (p. 68). What this means for us as home educators is that we not only need to provide the space and opportunity for free play but use that opportunity to keenly observe our children.

My 3-year-old brings me her fifth stuffed animal, a horse whose name today is Nola, explaining she has a cut hoof. She has already fixed Piggie's stomachache, Pup-pup's hurt tail, Husky's sprained foot, and Snowy the owl's broken wing. Tomorrow, instead of staying inside to play with her animals, she'll come out with my husband and I when our vet comes for our goats' wellness check-up. This is observation that meets curation. If she shows the same interests five years from now, I might ask the vet to talk to her a bit more about animals and what she does as a vet. This interest might fizzle out, but if not, curation snowballs into more in-depth opportunities to learn and then authentically apply her interests and build knowledge.

The coaching aspect integrates here in the ways I interact in play, if at all. Montessori would reprimand me for interrupting free play, but if play with me is sought out, I might "coach" by handing my daughter her vet kit, exploring the different tools and thinking aloud as to their purpose. *I wonder if these tweezers might take a tick out of our doggie friend's fur if we use them carefully?* In an overt way, we are coaching our way to expanding our children's vocabulary and schema—the fundamental building blocks to literacy.

A pause here to make a note of play for play's sake is imperative. While we might be in "education mode," particularly as a homeschooler, our children also *need* cognitive breaks. The need for play with zero educational intention is necessary. Put the ABC bath letters down. Laugh. Smile. Sometimes just engage in and with the environment simply out of joy vs. educational intent. In fact, practice joy and living most of the time. Education through apprenticeship will have many organic opportunities. It need not be forced.

It is through this kind of curation, collaboration, communication, coaching, and observation that we can begin to build out curriculum without it ever coming to fruition on paper as a structured approach. Instead of purchasing a scripted curriculum or a guide (not that that's bad to do), we use our observations of our children's interests to generate ever deeper quests for knowledge and skill, juggling multiple interests when we have multiple kids. Don't forget to involve the children in their own learning! How often have you found that the coursework you have experienced, however well-intentioned, did not pertain to you?

The most challenging aspect of learning is usually motivation. Interesting, because humans generally are an incredibly curious species. Motivation is tied to interest, authenticity, applicability, and audience. First, the interest. I very much like reading dystopian literature. The authenticity is in the value of what Rosenblatt (1995) calls aesthetic reading or reading for pleasure. I don't need to answer questions about what the color of the curtains were on page 57 after I read the book. I get lost in the flow of reading, experience emotion when I read, and my gravitation towards dystopian literature also doubles as preparation for a possible doomsday apocalypse (joking, kind of). The applicability of the experience is self-care; this is how I wind down and experience joy. In this case, my audience is me, myself, and I, but since I teach literature and humanities classes at college level in addition to teacher preparation coursework in literacy and young adult literature, there are also professional applications in that I continue to expand my working knowledge of dystopian young adult literature.

When we use scripted curriculum (again, not a bad thing, as long as we adapt towards interests and our unique children), what happens to motivation? We ask our children to engage in a topic that might be interesting to *us* or that we know will "benefit them," but they might not have any interest in the topic. The authenticity of the task is lacking. Are we able to connect X topic to the real world? Applicability typically goes hand in hand with authenticity. Can our children use this skill *in a way that they are able to perceive as beneficial in that moment*? Finally, audience. Who is the audience? Is the goal to appease the educator, regardless of who that is? Authentic learning happens when the audience, perceived or not, is engaged too. That is why publication is a crucial aspect of writing engagement; not in books or journals or the like but rather a publication for an audience that matters to the child. In early childhood, this is fairly easy—mom and dad are the audience. *Look at me, mama!* As children grow older, their need for audience shifts from solely mom and dad and possibly nuclear family to peers and a broader world. Technology, in this case, can be an incredible connector. Developmentally, this usually occurs between 5th and 8th grade.

As parents, we are the ultimate apprenticeship. The crux of it is that it is our jobs as parent-educators to be well informed to provide an education in this way. Well informed does not mean the all-knowing. It does not necessitate a doctorate. As an aside, I know plenty of people with doctorates who lack common sense. Well informed might mean deeply knowledgeable about a content area or two, a skill, a trade, or a profession. It also means well informed of who else might be a positive and significant role model and mentor for your children. It means well informed in your own value system and your own biases, as well as your own strengths and weaknesses. Just as we will learn a lot from observing our children, our children will learn a lot from observing us.

In my experience, one of the best ways to stay informed and passionate about learning is to read. I read just about anything I can get my hands on. I binge read a genre, then move to another, sometimes circling back to reread some of my favorite novels, including the Harry Potter series. A tangential note on rereading; it is an incredibly great way to build reading fluency, and we are never the same person twice, so rereading a text might be a wholly new experience the second (or third, or fourth) time around. My husband, on the other hand, is not an avid reader. He prefers to *do*. He has built every outbuilding on our land by hand, meticulously measuring, cutting, sawing, drilling, doing, *learning*. I have made a career out of words. He has made a career out of wood.

The need to stay informed in some fashion—to continue to learn about life and living it—does not end with the culmination of homeschooling. The apprenticeship between a parent and a child is a challenge as the goalposts are constantly moving. A mother gives birth to a daughter who will transform her mother into a grandmother, bringing life upon life upon life—

these humans will learn from each other what it means to be a mom, a daughter, and a grandmother. While a state department of education might deem it important for a homeschooling family to cover science, math, social studies, English, and health, the apprenticeship does not end (or begin) in siloed, watered-down pockets of knowledge about the world. The apprenticeship model knows no curriculum and deems important what the family deems important. Let's put our phones down, and find, once again, our joy in curiosity, as this will inevitably bring joy in learning about the world.

***

I sat down with the 3rd grade teacher to discuss her worksheet woes. We talked about positive ways to communicate with the parent about the harms of being digitally distracted. We landed on a solution—the child really loved to read one particular book. The child would come home that day with the worksheet and a note attached to that book—a gift, to be read at home however many times they wanted to, together.

 ## Do Something

- Consider your family's top three values and engage in a conversation about how you all model those values.
- Set aside time for yourself to engage in what you find informative, then, if you are enthusiastic about it, share that learning with your family.
- A valuable learning experience almost always begins with an authentic, real-world question. Consider the many questions you or your children or family have about the world. Write them down on sticky notes and explore them together.
- Ask around within your learning co-op, among friends, colleagues, or family—what do you feel you are an expert in? Make a note of what everyone says for future reference. Grandma might know how to knit a beautiful stocking out of yarn; a good friend might know how to make some wicked good whoopie pie; a colleague might

be an avid bird watcher or know the specifics about income taxes; a local 5-year-old might be able to tell you the names of various dinosaurs.

◆ Dedicate time to formal instruction if you wish, but also dedicate time simply to find joy in living with no educational intention. The irony is often these moments are the most educational of all but cannot be forced.

◆ If there were no subject areas but rather fundamental skills that help a child become successful in life, what would they be? How are you and your family going to model and attend to these fundamentals?

References

Britannica. (2021). *Plato summary*. Encyclopedia Britannica. https://www.britannica.com/summary/Plato

Dennen, V., & Burner, K.J. (2008). *The cognitive apprenticeship model in educational practice*. Retrieved December 20, 2021, from https://faculty.weber.edu/eamsel/Classes/Projects%20and%20Research%20(4800)/Teaching%20and%20Learning/Dennen%20&%20Burner%20(2008).pdf

Doucleff, M. (2021). *Hunt, gather, parent*. Avid Reader Press/Simon & Schuster.

Fuller, A., & Unwin, L. (2011). Apprenticeship as an evolving model of learning. *Journal of Vocational Education and Training, 63*(3), 261–266.

Gatto, J.T. (2017). *Dumbing us down: The hidden curriculum of compulsory schooling*. New Society Publishers.

Heying, H., & Weinstein, B. (2021). *A hunter gatherer's guide to the 21st century: Evolution and the challenges of modern life*. Penguin.

Katz, M. (1976a). The origins of public education: A reassessment. *History of Education Quarterly, 16*(4), 381–407.

Katz, M. (1976b). *A history of compulsory education laws*. Retrieved December 20, 2021, from https://files.eric.ed.gov/fulltext/ED119389.pdf

King, B. (2012). *For how long have we been human?* Retrieved December 20, 2021, from https://www.npr.org/sections/13.7/2012/09/11/160934187/for-how-long-have-we-been-human

Kober, N. (2020). *History and evolution of public education in the US.* Retrieved December 20, 2021, from Center on Education Policy, Graduate School of Education and Human Development, The George Washington University https://files.eric.ed.gov/fulltext/ED606970.pdf

Messerli, J. (1972). *Horace Mann: A biography.* Knopf.

Montessori, M. (1986). *Discovery of the child.* Mass Market Paperback.

Robinson, S.K. (2010). *Changing education paradigms.* Retrieved December 20, 2021, from https://www.ted.com/talks/sir_ken_robinson_changing_education_paradigms

Robinson, S.K. (2017). *Out of our minds: The power of being creative.* John Wiley and Sons Ltd.

Rosenblatt, L. (1995). *Literature as exploration.* Modern Language Association.

Wagner, T., & Dintersmith, T. (2015). *Most likely to succeed: Preparing our kids for the innovation era.* Scribner.

5

Self-Directed Education

An Interview with Dr. Peter Gray

Katie Rybakova Mathews

Popular texts about homeschooling, including *The Call of the Wild and Free* (Arment, 2019), *Sage Homeschooling* (Rainbolt, 2017), and *Unschooling* (McDonald, 2019), have a commonality—they all cite Dr. Peter Gray, a research professor at Boston College and author of *Free to Learn: Why Unleashing the Instinct to Play Will Make Our Children Happier, More Self-Reliant, and Better Students for Life* (2015). For good reason too: Gray is an expert in psychology and has focused a major part of his career on self-directed and play-based learning, as well as evolutionary, developmental, and educational psychology. In short, he knows what he is talking about. Perhaps the most compelling instance in his book *Free to Learn* (Gray, 2015) comes from his own personal experiences sending his son to the Sudbury Valley School in Massachusetts, an interesting enigma of brick and mortar institutions where students, rather than teachers, lead curricular pursuits. Additional aspects of his book often cited are his descriptions of how play is defined through a psychological lens. Still other aspects of the book include an anthropological lens, where we are reminded that we share the same genetic code as hunter–gatherers, and that we have a lot to learn from the play-rich, mixed age environment

DOI: 10.4324/9781003267362-5

of modern-day hunter–gatherers. This sentiment is echoed by more recent texts such as *Hunt, Gather, Parent* (Doucleff, 2021).

It is no wonder that many unschooling families gravitate to Gray's notions of child-directed play and self-directed education. His vision of self-directed education is even broader than the unschooling philosophy in many ways, in the sense that it can, for the most part, be truly for everyone and every family in some form. The following interview was edited for clarity and length.

Katie Rybakova Mathews (KR): You have published often since *Free to Learn*. Have you found that unschooling as a philosophy has shifted or changed?

Peter Gray (PG): *My focus is on self-directed education whether it is occurring through unschooling or any kind of school that is designed for self-directed education, such as a Sudbury school or agile learning center. I did not start off with a particular interest in unschooling. What changed my career was a study of the graduates of the Sudbury Valley School. I became interested in how they were learning without any curriculum. This led to an interest in how learning occurs through children's play and exploration. Children come into the world biologically designed to educate themselves, and we, as parents, need to provide the condition to do so.*

I have not been part of the debates within unschoolers. I wrote about the results of an article that Gina Riley and I published on my Psychology Today blog regarding unschooling. We conducted a study of unschooling families and asked participants to describe what unschooling was to them and how they did it. Moms that gave authority to the children for their own education and did the least in terms of monitoring what they were learning we called radical unschooling. I quickly learned from very strong-minded people that radical unschooling has a different definition. A radical unschooling family applies the philosophy of not directing your children to all of their lives. The parent would not ask the children to do chores. Instead, they might have a discussion about what and how chores are completed as a family.

Unschooling as a philosophy should have less doctrine. Families may differ and that is okay. One of the things that

I promote is to try and get over the terminology of unschooling. It's such a negative term. It tells people what you're not doing. It sets school up to be defensive because it sounds like you're rejecting what they're doing. Many people equate schooling with education; it sounds like you're against education. I promote the terminology of self-directed education, partly to unite the people who have traditionally called themselves unschoolers and register as homeschoolers, along with the people who are sending their child to a school or a learning center that's designed for self-directed education, like a Sudbury school.

The other reason for savoring that term is that education is a word that has a halo around it in our culture and it is very important that people understand that homeschoolers are not rejecting the idea of education. We simply have a different idea about how education best occurs, and that it is stickier when children are in charge of the education process for themselves. To gain mainstream acceptance it is important that we use positive terms. It is hard to get away from unschooling because it has become so much a part of the vocabulary of people doing it. There are other terms as well, such as relaxed homeschoolers or eclectic homeschoolers. Doctrinaire thinking—that you're almost evil if you insist that your child wash dishes—is not as common as an attitude that there are many ways to unschool.

KR: How does unstructured play tie into self-directed education?

PG: *There is no such thing as unstructured play. All play is structured and structured by the players themselves. It is not a random activity; when you are playing you are doing something structured. A play fight may look unstructured but is structured in a certain sense. It has rules. The rules might not be stated, but, for instance, you cannot really hurt the other person. One of the amazing, wonderful things about players is how children learn to structure their own activities. A part of the definition of play is it is freely chosen. You are free to quit.*

In my book I talked about three instincts that drive play. One of them is curiosity, which is the drive to explore. We come into the world very curious and you cannot stop it. This begins in youth. What can I do with it? Will it break if I drop it on the floor? What will happen if I stick my finger in this electric socket? That is part of how we educate ourselves. The primary function of curiosity is to gain information about the world, and thus constantly exploring that world is crucial to learning.

Play is doing things. Play is acting on things in certain ways. I argue that there are two parts to education; one is acquiring information, and the other is acquiring skills. Curiosity is the drive to acquire information to figure out how it works. Children come into the world biologically designed to play with all the skills that are important for people to learn. For instance, they play through physical activities, because you need to learn how to control your body. No matter where children are born, they play with language. Nobody teaches children their native language.

Children everywhere play imaginative games. We are the animal that can imagine—this is what we call hypothetical thinking. This thinking involves imagination. Children want to play mostly with other children. They are learning how to get along with peers. They are learning how to negotiate how to get their needs met while still meeting the needs of their peers. They are learning how to make friends. It is not surprising that in the course of natural selection children would have evolved a drive to play, and particularly an ability to take control of their own lives—to initiate activities, to solve their own problems— because in play they are responsible to solve their own problems. If there is an adult there, they are solving their problems for them.

The third drive is associative ability. Associative ability goes beyond social curiosity. Children are naturally drawn to other people; they want to know what other people know. Whether or not you are deliberately teaching them, they are learning from you by watching you and overhearing you. Children learn much more by eavesdropping than they do through lecture.

Sometimes I have been misrepresented as saying play is the sole focus of education, but I have never said that. I distinguish between play and exploration. Children are drawn to other humans and learn naturally from other humans.

KR: We are so used to doing the adult-directed play setup for children. What is the parent's role in a conducive environment for play?

PG: *When I grew up in the 1950s, parents did not have to do any-*
thing except send children outdoors. Every parent did that. As a
consequence, all the kids were outdoors if they were not in school.
I know this was true in every neighborhood, as I moved around
a lot as a child. I lived in cities, I lived in villages—you could go
outdoors any time of day and there were other kids to play with.
Children would play in vacant lots, streets, playgrounds, lakes,
and woods. Nobody stopped children's play time other than for
dinner. Sadly, we do not live in that world anymore. Parents
are over-protective of their children; they do not just send their
child outside. Our society has become such that those parents
who do send their child outside worry that they will be arrested.
Moreover, if the child goes out, there may not be anybody to play
with. Children get their cell phone out and communicate with
friends the only way they can because they are not outdoors to
play with. That is the world we are in. That does create a job for
parents. If you want your child to play, the primary stimulus for
play is other children. The more other children the child has the
option to play with, the more likely the child will make friends.

People with large families say this kind of play can happen
among siblings. That is true to a degree, but there is a difference
between play with siblings and play with people who are not
siblings. You have to earn your friends. Your siblings are there
no matter what. You can bully them if you want.

Homeschoolers try to provide opportunities where home-
schooling families get together and the kids know one another.
The challenge is that children need time to play with no adult
there telling them what to do. In this world it is going to be hard
to get kids together with parent permission unless there is an
adult there. It is very important that we have adults who know
how to be there without being there. Allow children to climb
trees. Allow them to wrestle. Allow them to teach one another, to
disagree, and even fight a little bit, recognizing that this is how
children learn and play. They learn how to resolve their own
problems. They learn courage by climbing trees. They learn how
to deal with people not always being nice to them by recognizing
that people are not always nice. It does not necessarily mean that
some parent has to swoop in and rescue the child.

KR: Homeschooling is still stigmatized. How do you think you would talk back to the criticisms of homeschooling?

PG: *I believe homeschooling is stigmatized less now than it was some years ago, largely because more and more people are doing it. I presented data from the US census bureau on a blog post in Psychology Today from May 2021. Almost 20% of American families with school aged children were homeschooling. Social psychologists call that percentage the tipping point, which indicates how a phenomenon moves from atypical to socially acceptable. If this percentage were to remain, homeschooling no longer seems like a weird thing to do. We do not know how many people are going to keep homeschooling if the COVID-19 threat subsides, but anecdotally those who were pressed into homeschooling because of COVID-19 are likely to stick with it. Parents and professional organizations that I have spoken to comment that their children are happy and seem to be learning.*

During the lockdown period from school parents learned things about school and about their own child, which led them to question the value of school for their child. Some of them were monitoring the distance learning. They began to think—why is that so important? They noticed their child was not interested in the subject material but was interested in something else. Schools cannot accommodate to children's individual interests. At home, it is possible.

I conducted a study with colleagues on how families adapted during the pandemic. The study had a demographically balanced national sample. What we found was that early on in the pandemic, children reported themselves less anxious and happier than they were prior to the lockdown. This reads counter to what most people predicted, and still counter to what we commonly read in the popular press. There were three other studies conducted at the same time that showed a similar result. Children were doing better at home than they were in school. It is not surprising because of the evidence that we already had. School is a major source of anxiety, depression, and even suicide among school-aged children.

Some parents had a child with a special-needs diagnosis. They had been fighting the school to try and get the school to meet their needs. Schools have curricula to support special needs, but they almost never work. The school cannot meet the needs of the child, and furthermore, the school ends up isolating and stigmatizing the child. At home, education can be designed according to the child's needs.

I think we are going to leave the COVID-19 period with a greater acceptance of homeschooling because there will be more people who are aware of it.

KR: How should families who are saying yes, we're going to homeschool, decide if unschooling or self-directed education is the right choice for their family?

PG: *What I would define as self-directed education works for essentially every child. There may be some cases—for example, somebody who is very far out on the autism spectrum who does not naturally play— where those educative drives are lacking. This is not inclusive of the great bulk of people who get called autistic and are simply a little odd socially, or children who do not make easy personal connections. Those people often do very well with self-directed education; in some sense they need it because they need their own space. Some children need to meet people on their own terms rather than be forced into forming relationships.*

There is not a personality type for which self-directed education works better. A lot of people think some children are self-motivated and others are not. Show me a three-year-old who is not self-motivated. We are always trying to stop their self-motivation!

Some people see their own child come home from school and flop down in front of the TV. They look passive and as if they are not doing anything. This situation is very similar to an adult who comes home from a hard day at work. They are exhausted and frustrated, and they do the same thing—they flop down in front of the TV. School is not the solution—school is creating that mood. There are some people who need to get out of school more than others, for whom there is obvious damage. There are children who fight and resist school. They are the ones who get diagnosed with ADHD. They do not thrive in school. These are children who need to get out of school because they are unhappy in school.

In general children are adaptive and there are not a lot of children in school suffering in an immediate sense. However, in the long run, they are still suffering, even the ones who are getting A's. They are growing up in an environment in which the fundamental thing they are learning is that whatever they do they are doing for the sake of the judgement that comes from somebody else. Children learn to grow up with a sense of self-judgement by virtue of how other people judge them. They judge whether an activity is worthwhile based on what others think, rather than judging it on the basis of whether or not they would find enjoyment in it. A lot of people who look very successful in school may end up in jobs that look like great success, but as a consequence we have a lot of very unhappy doctors and lawyers. They never had the opportunity to play and discover what they really like to do. They lived a life that seems like going through one hoop after another. As adults they might point to fiscal success, but the question remains of whether or not they feel happy. Are they living the life that they really would want to live? Some of them are, but a lot of them are not. Self-directed education is for everybody. Self-directed education is very different from person to person because we are all different.

Some people might, in a very self-directed way, say "I want courses." If they are choosing the courses and they can quit whenever they want, as occurs at a Sudbury type school—that's self-directed. They are choosing that. Some people like structure. That is part of self-directed education. If you like structure, you can choose structure—as long as that is your choice.

There are also people who go in and out of school. A child might tell a parent that they want to try school. I think it would be very wrong for the parent to say, "No, you are not allowed to try school because school is evil and bad." The right thing to say is, "Sure, try it, just know you can quit whenever you want, as long as this is your choice." Nine times out of ten a child can go right into an age-related grade level and not feel behind in anything, not because they learned anything but because nobody has learned very much.

Humans are social by nature and we want to connect with other people we care about. We care about what other people *think. Simultaneously, we recognize from a very early age that we are responsible for ourselves. This is true even of very little children, such as toddlers. Toddlers seem to say no to everything new because we are asking them to do it. They know at some level of their being that they have to take charge of their own life and that they are ultimately responsible for their own life. I add a fourth educative drive, which is willfulness. The child is willful. The child wants to do what the child wants to do, and that is how children learn to take charge of their own life. They want to resist control. That is true of every normal child. The child who says "I really want somebody who knows how to play the violin to give me violin lessons" is very different from the child whose parents say, "You have to take violin lessons."*

KR: That speaks to the next question—those who self-direct their learning who go on to a more formal, traditional setting—it sounds like it is because they want to, so they do not have as much difficulty adjusting.

PG: *Some of my research has been on grown unschoolers and graduates of the Sudbury Valley School, and more recently, the graduates of another school modeled after Sudbury Valley. They do not have any difficulty going to college. That was the most surprising finding to me. Children who have never been to school or never taken a course can get into college, and, at least in this country, they can succeed. In fact, I became convinced that they may even have an advantage.*

Imagine what a boring job it must be to be an admissions counselor at a place like Harvard or Stanford. Every single application seems perfect: the applicant has high test scores, has taken all honors classes, has completed all of the "right" extracurricular activities, and has written the perfect essay. Then, an application comes in where the student has written that they have not had any formal schooling, but then lists out what they have accomplished. They write authentically about why they want to go to that school, and their essay seems genuine. You can't just throw that in the wastebasket.

One of the characteristics of people who grow up with self-directed education is that they tend to be very good at interviews. They are not afraid of adults. They are full of questions. They know how to stand up for themselves. They have a story to tell. That is the case for a certain number that I know of who went directly from self-directed education to a highly competitive college.

More commonly, a child would have taken a few community college courses before applying to college. By the time they are 16, they can take a course or two from a local community college. Community colleges often have an array of subjects, cost little, and there are few admissions requirements. After these courses, a child can show that they have taken a few formal courses and done well. The great majority of cases—they have been at the grade they would have been in and they do fine. We tend to think of education as cumulative—you have to learn A before you learn B before you learn C. But the truth of the matter is, that is not the case.

References

Arment, A. (2019). *The call of the wild and free: Reclaiming the wonder in your child's education*. HarperOne.

Doucleff, M. (2021). *Hunt, gather, parent*. Avid Reader Press/Simon & Schuster.

Gray, P. (2015). *Free to learn: Why unleashing the instinct to play will make our children happier, more self-reliant, and better students for life*. Basic Books.

McDonald, K. (2019). *Unschooled: Raising curious, well-educated children outside the conventional classroom*. Chicago Review Press Inc.

Rainbolt, R. (2017). *Sage homeschooling*. Create Space Independent Publishing Platform.

Interlude

The Science Behind Nature-based Learning

Michael R. Barnes

Nature has a fundamental impact on the well-being, learning, and development of children. The concept of nature-based learning (NBL) encompasses a wide variety of contexts in which learning and development are enhanced by children being in and engaging with the natural world. Thus it incorporates broad definitions of both *nature* and *learning*.

Nature can include water, sand, soil, vegetation, animals, insects, and other natural materials that can be found across diverse landscapes from nearby urban parks to remote wilderness areas. While nature can be *wilderness* in the image of U.S. national parks like Yellowstone or Joshua Tree, it can also be right outside your doorstep, whether that be a yard, a neighborhood park, or a community garden. The best nature is nature that's *accessible* to you.

Learning not only includes traditional aspects of acquiring and retaining knowledge but also the development and cultivation of skills (e.g., leadership), attitudes, values, and behaviors that can persist into the future. Learning can be formal, such as a biology lesson taking place at a pond with a set curriculum, informal like a parent–child nature walk, or completely self-directed where a child explores and interacts with worms after it rains in the backyard.

DOI: 10.4324/9781003267362-6

These broad definitions of nature and learning and subsequently NBL allow for a more complete understanding of the critical and positive relationships between nature and children that decades of research have identified. The next section will provide a brief overview of the many benefits of NBL for children (and parents).

Attention & Stress Relief

Nature-based learning has demonstrated clearly that time spent in nature can help to improve and restore attentional resources as well as relieve stress. Individuals have a certain amount of attentional resources to draw from before they become attentionally fatigued. Nature via multiple pathways helps to restore those attentional resources, allowing us the ability to focus and direct our attention to the task at hand. Children can benefit from nature exposure in the learning context, especially those who might struggle with focusing in a traditional classroom environment such as students with ADHD. Even viewing nature from a window can help restore attentional resources. Nature helps reduce stress in a similar manner being easier to understand than built spaces, as well as being away from spaces that are stress-inducing.

As little as 10-15 minutes of being in or viewing nature can have restorative effects for attention and stress relief.

Motivation & Engagement

Sometimes the biggest barrier for a child is being motivated and engaged long enough to be able to learn the material in front of them. Several types of NBL have been found to improve students' motivation for learning, which is thought to be due to nature's effect on mood. It makes sense that a child who's feeling more positive would be more open to learning. Critically,

NBL enhances a child's *intrinsic* motivation for learning; said differently, nature drives a motivation for learning that isn't dependent on external rewards but rather an internal motivation to learn. Additionally, NBL has been shown to increase student engagement with activities and lessons which in turn improves learning outcomes.

> *Different natural spaces might motivate children differently, so if one type isn't working, try a different landscape if possible.*

Warmer & Cooperative Relationships

Nature helps foster relationships among children and between children and adults. Nature-based learning experiences help to bridge a variety of barriers that can influence the development of bonds between peers and child–adult relationships. The freedom afforded by nature aids in facilitating more open and genuine interactions between children, which can encourage cooperation, teamwork, and build friendships. Nature-based learning also assists in overcoming traditional social and cultural barriers that can sometimes limit a child's inclusion in social activities. Child–adult interactions are also affected, as nature seems to bridge the authority gap by providing a space where children and adults are learning together on a similar level akin to peer learning.

> *Enhancing cooperation and the relationships within a learning community can assist in improving academic outcomes.*

Creativity & Autonomy

Nature affords children the physical materials known as *loose parts* (e.g., rocks, sticks, dirt, water) that encourage child-led creative play styles. These natural loose parts allow children to express themselves in more creative ways and socialize with other children through diverse forms of play that encourage cooperation and physical activity. An important aspect of nature-based play is that it helps children develop a sense of autonomy, which plays a role in fostering self-confidence and a child's identity.

A loose parts bin, inside or outside, can be a great addition to an at-home learning environment, especially when getting outside or to a desired natural area is difficult.

Learning & Development

All of the previously mentioned benefits of NBL work via multiple pathways to improve a child's learning and development. These outcomes can be specific and acute, such as increasing how much information from a lesson is retained or improvements in quiz scores. However, NBL can have impacts on learning further in the future related to standardized test scores and high school graduation rates. It can also affect children's development of skills that might be critical to future success, such as critical thinking, communication, teamwork, and individual resilience. Finally, NBL connects children with the natural world and fosters stewardship values that can persist and influence pro-environmental behaviors into adulthood.

Taken together, the effects of NBL on children's learning and development is significant and wide-reaching. It can also be a way to level the playing field in learning and development for children of diverse backgrounds, learning styles, and other differences that might cause a child to struggle in traditional learning environments. Nature, whether outside your doorstep or a world away, can truly be a place where children feel at peace while learning and growing in ways that match their unique needs and skills.

6

Wildschooling

Nicolette Sowder

There is typically one definitive moment when each family real-izes that they will be home educating their child. But before that crystalized revelation, every family (whether consciously observed or not) has their series of thoughts and events that lead up to that life-altering decision. In our particular story, the fundamental experiences that brought us to that threshold were steeped in nature.

When my firstborn was one year old, my husband and I purchased a rundown farm in Michigan. We had never been so completely surrounded by the wild. And we had never felt so overwhelmed by the responsibilities that come with being first-time parents and farmers. There was so much to fix, both inside and out. We would come to find that healing was at the center of our journey and purpose.

The idea of "healing the land" is a colonized perspective. After eight years on this sacred ground, we now know that we were projecting our own wounds onto the landscape. What we came to heal would ultimately heal us. Our deepest disconnects and opportunities for inner repair emerged in tandem with our daughter's natural curiosity and kinship with her environment. Where she moved in closer to animals and plants, we worried and hesitated. Where she wanted to climb and dig, we balked and held back.

DOI: 10.4324/9781003267362-7

It became painfully evident that we did not know this place, truer still we did not know ourselves in relationship to its wonder and offerings. There was no way out but through, so we started to rebuild that trust with each other and all the creatures around us. This relational recentering transformed our entire world. Our senses activated, curiosity ignited, and instincts awakened. What was once perceived as danger, fear, and otherness, was replaced with a familial connection and comforting truth—we weren't doing this alone. We were co-parenting with Mother Nature.

With this renewed support, my daughter began to flourish. She danced and sang across meadows, foraged for herbs and berries, ran in the rain, became friends with the forest, and played in all weather. We wandered and wondered our way through our days with full feeling. And then she turned five. The quickly-approaching train of traditional schooling and all it demanded was headed right towards us—a ride that once boarded, would be almost impossible to get off. So when it stopped at our door, we simply let it go right by.

This act was simultaneously one of the easiest yet most difficult decisions we've ever made. Easy because for the last four years we had been learning, growing, and unfurling in a diverse, stimulating ecosystem. Leaving that state of being for a more limited one wasn't an option at that point. But hard because aspects of the path ahead were brambled and unknown. It was out of this fruitful darkness, like a mushroom appearing raising up from soil, that Wildscholing emerged.

The Wildschooling Way

Our family had left the classroom behind and I was programmed to think we had to enter into something else. As it turns out, it wasn't so much an entrance as an acknowledgment of the rich continuum, path, and personhood that my daughter was already deeply living and becoming. Inseparable from our environment, we called our way of walking "wildschooling." Wildschooling is a home education framework rooted in our innate, inexorable bond with Mother Nature. This way of being is rooted in honoring the whole child, village rhythm, orientation to local biome, and wildness-as-relationship as our human birthright.

I started writing as a way of documenting this process of deep co-connection with Earth. These reflections resonated with thousands of families around the world. In that way, wildschooling is a movement and way of being created with countless caregivers, all of whom are answering a deep call within themselves—a call to come back into the circle of wild things. Access and connection to nature is not just a "nice to have," it's a necessity. This perspective and understanding is hardly new. For 200,000 years of human history, we have lived and grown in mutual relationship with the land. Countless studies show that learning alongside and in context with nature is where our brains and bodies develop best. Indoor education is a relatively new experiment—an experiment that risks the health and happiness of every child kept within its walls.

Decolonizing Homeschooling

No one knows this reality better than Indigenous Peoples who have tended the land since time immemorial, before having their birthright and homeland stripped from them. Wildschooling is a movement predicated on freedom and inclusion, rooting itself in a decolonized vision of homeschooling. At the root of reconciliation is the promise of a place-bonded movement that reflects the biodiverse, resilient, creative, and transformative power of nature itself. That requires actively honoring and supporting Indigenous Peoples who have deep cultural roots and rights to the land. It must include supporting the relatives of those enslaved peoples who have been historically disenfranchised and denied access to land rights and green spaces.

Nature and place-based pedagogy did not simply manifest out of thin air. These ideas are an echo of the traditional and cultural inheritance from those whose voices have been erased from the record for far too long.

I am located in North America, specifically Western Michigan; ancestral, traditional, and contemporary lands of the Anishinaabeg–Three Fires Confederacy of Ojibwe, Odawa, and

Potawatomi peoples. Tribes are not monoliths and the best way to learn is to go to the Indigenous Peoples' organizations and representatives in your specific region. From my own perspective, these local connections have helped me move from a place of egocentric, commodified ownership over the land to one of mutual, reciprocal kinship. Indigenous land-bonded education goes far beyond "outdoor education." It asks us to look underneath the layers of contemporary practice to the culture-rich soil beneath. In practice this can look like learning the original language of the land, creating mixed-age, elder-inclusive spaces, respectfully practicing and learning traditional craft, "wild" food and medicine preparation, and sharing stories around a real or proverbial fire. Essentially, it looks less like "taking the classroom outside" and more like the ancient dance and way of being to which we're aligned. It looks like life.

Where to Start

Those families looking to get started homeschooling will most likely turn to the Internet for a roadmap. There they find a wide range of information, philosophies, and perspectives. In my case, I was filled with a growing sense of urgency and desperation to choose a curriculum, something that could guide and help me make sure that my daughter wouldn't be "left behind." So of course, I started purchasing and testing bundles, worksheets, and entire frameworks. Time and time again, life would interest and call to us infinitely more than any predefined road or method of instruction. Instead of fighting what was coming naturally, we went with the flow. And we were not alone. I was bolstered by thousands of other families all over the world learning in "non-traditional" ways. Unschooling in particular centered on sovereignty in a way that resonated. Holt's (1990) powerful concept of "deschooling" forced me to look at the patterns, habits, and ideas that my 18 plus years in the traditional school system had entrenched in me.

So much of my deconstruction was being done outside. Mother Nature was there helping to hold me together as I examined deeply held beliefs that felt inextricable from my core identity. Amongst the giant oaks, flowers, hawks, and honeybees, "deschooling" no longer encompassed all I was experiencing. Closer to the feeling was a re-initiation into a sphere of life and wisdom that included, but wasn't limited to, human understanding. It was a homecoming. Wildschooling's process of entering back into the rhythms, cycles, and pulse of ALL of life is called *Rejoining*.

Rejoining has no set beginning and end, but I recommend it span at least one entire seasonal year, from winter solstice to the following winter solstice. During that time, the intention is to reattune together as a family. Get curious, engage your senses, explore, and be open to experiencing nature's changeable aspects. Follow the moon, play in all weather, get dirty, and just BE. The opposite of *Rejoining* is isolation, confinement inside of the sphere of human concern and direction. In that state, interactions with nature are primarily one-sided and commodified. Once we remember our nature-bonded inheritance and place in the circle, nature no longer becomes a place to be or thing to use, but a partner in transformation. A huge indicator that a family has moved towards this transition is that time in nature no longer feels transactional, but instead becomes relational. That often results in a focus and experiences that are less "activity-based" and more contextual. For example, flowers for a craft might be approached in seasonal alignment and using principles from the Honorable Harvest (Kimmerer, 2015), as opposed to mindlessly gathered.

Wildschooling Architecture

Often when people ask me about wildschooling, they want to know particulars. The beauty of this way is that there are no set rules, only suggestions. There is no WRONG way to wildschool. It can be done in any biome, city, suburb, or country. Cityscapes contain many rich opportunities to engage with nature and in some cases have more access to communal gardens and programs. Families do not need to own their own land or house. There is no specific set of abilities or background required. Each biome, caregiver, child, and condition is unique and it is that diversity which makes the whole of the wildschooling community stronger. Unschooling and some other eclectic homeschooling methods do not have any particular start or end date to the educational year. In wildschooling, it is recommended to begin at a key seasonal point and end at that same point the following year. This year represents one year, one turn of the seasonal, solar wheel. Rather than an endless, unending span of time, humans evolved observing and marking seasonal, astronomical cycles. Anchoring to these points helps children fall into a natural rhythm and creates a sense of safety and flow.

We personally begin on winter solstice and end on winter solstice the following year. In this way, as the sun's strength grows, so too does our knowledge. We mark our movements, growth, and experience at the lunar cycles and eight seasonal points (winter solstice, midpoint between winter and spring, spring equinox, midpoint between spring and summer, summer solstice, midpoint between summer and fall, fall equinox, midpoint between fall and winter) serving as guideposts. Instead of letting any one resource guide the trajectory and direction of the whole of that year, the child and family's leg of their journey is considered central.

Wildschooling is not anti-curriculum. Some families follow a more traditional curriculum, while some take a mix and match approach. But the hope is that Wildschoolers maintain an emergent, village-led perspective. That is, look to their own biome, communal, and contextual needs and pull from the resources to fulfill those needs, as opposed to letting the curriculum "walk" the child. By studying nature's calendar and embracing the dynamic culture that arises from observing seasonal points and rhythms, life and focus reveals itself more authentically.

Pillars

In lieu of a set curriculum, wildschooling has a set of living pillars to help guide its community.

Wildschooling Recognizes Nature Connection as a Fundamental Human Need, Right, and State of Being

We are hard-wired to evolve with nature. We are nature! Nature connection is a developmental and emotional need for children, keying up biological functions that would otherwise be latent. Wildschooling recognizes and champions the need for ALL children to safely access and reconnect to their wild.

Wildschooling Values and Respects the Sovereign Rights of the Whole Child

Wildschooling values and trusts the child's need for unique self-expression; the right to move, unfurl, and process at their own pace. It honors the thousand languages of the child and supports the child's fundamental need to grow and develop through risk, play, experimentation, conversation, visceral sensory stimuli, and real, tangible life experiences.

Wildschooling Is Relationship Led

Time in nature isn't a curriculum extension, backdrop for activities, or afterthought. The nature–child connection is a living, breathing relationship. One that has innate value and meaning in and of itself. This lifelong dynamic, reciprocal dance between the wild and the child is the beating heart of wildschooling.

Wildschooling Favors Place-Bonded, Contextual, and Emergent Learning

Children must be given the time, space, and opportunity to connect to the outside world. The simplest, most meaningful, and effective place to do that is for them to connect to their local habitat, biome, backyard, and nearby nature. Further inquiry and supporting education serves those needs, questions, and sparks that arise.

Wildschooling Aligns with Nature's Rhythms

Wildschooling keeps time with the slower, more intentional rhythms of nature. Instead of the clock, it invites the child to orient to the solar year, phenological events, circadian rhythms, and seasonal shifts. Tethering to nature's calendar allows us to recognize the non-linear, more cyclical nature of a child's development.

Wildschooling Is Village Led and Oriented

For thousands of years, human culture has been inextricably linked to nature. Wildschooling understands nature connection to be incomplete without a community within which to express it. Ideally children are playing and learning in mixed-age, diverse groups. Parents and trusted caretakers are not separated from the child's learning and life journey. Community events, volunteer projects, outreach, and local celebrations help the child to extend their sphere of concern, empathy, and passion.

Wildschooling Respects and Honors Indigenous and Ancestral Knowledge

The art of survival inspired and strengthened our ancestors' connection to their environment. Respectfully practicing (without appropriation) Indigenous, traditional, and creative arts helps children honor the past while fostering creativity, embodiment, and preparedness for the days ahead.

Wildschooling Preserves and Honors Storytelling

Sharing and receiving each other's stories is almost synonymous with being human. Consistently gathering around the fire (metaphorical or real) to partake in that ancient ritual is worth preserving. And when a Wildschooler walks away from the fire, others will be there to receive and integrate that story when that child returns.

Wildschooling Supports a Future Paradigm

Wildschoolers are dandelions bursting through the pavement. This type of approach to life and education aspires to help raise children who are flexible, creative, resilient, and empathetic. Although so many of wildschooling's tenants draw on the past, this approach can walk our children into their best future.

 **Do Something**

For those looking for more tangible aspects of the framework, there are several ways in which wildschooling can be reflected and supported.

◆ **The Wild Wheel**

The Wild Wheel is the centerpiece of our home. Its shape and orientation is a tangible way to help keep us tuned to a more circular, nature-bonded, and holistic sense of time. The Wild Wheel consists of a wreath made out of vine (or available materials). Four sticks are used to divide it into eight sections (one point for each astronomical touchpoint in the seasonal year). As the year progresses, a marker is moved around to indicate the general time in the season. Children can collect or make items that reflect repeated, culturally, or environmentally important moments of the year and affix them to that spot on the wheel. For example, when the birds start to migrate back to our region around March, we mark the moment on our wheel with a feather.

◆ **Book of Being**

The Book of Being is partly reflection of the Wild Wheel and partly a tool for deeper documentation. "The Book of Being" is an acknowledgment that children's lives are not products to be measured against an ever-moving target, but instead are journeys to be mapped. Each child (and adult if they so choose) has their own Book of Being. The purpose of each Book is to document the creativity, achievements, sparks, phenology, and wonder of the child's life. It can also be as inclusive of more structured curriculum and studies as each family would like.

One solar year (one turn of the wheel from winter solstice to winter solstice) equals one volume in the Book of Being. That volume is in a binder and contains dividers representing the eight astronomical points and lunar cycles. Materials, investigations, pictures, and observations are placed in the part of the seasonal year in which they emerged. This can be as simple or as complex as you like. When that solar year is done, all of its contents are removed and placed in the Book of Being (which is held in a large container). Then another volume is readied in preparation for another solar year.

◆ **Wildschooling Villages**

Wildschooling is fundamentally a community-centric movement with the land and relational bonds strengthened through shared connection. Wildschooling Villages were formed to help bring wildschooling families together within the context of their local environments and ecosystems. The culture of alloparenting, care, and support network that forms when we gather is what transforms this movement from theory to practice.

◆ **The Kids Moon Club**

For those looking for a guided experience in reconnection, The Kids Moon Club is a year-long, lunar-inspired membership. Through celebration, story, art, and food, its purpose is to help families and communities realign to nature's pace.

◆ **Create Your Moondala**

The new moon marks the beginning of every lunar cycle and initiates intention and dream-setting for our family. To do this, we print out our Moondalas, bring out art supplies, light a candle, and brew a cup of tea. Together, we draw and color our hopes for the 28-day cycle ahead. Please join us in this tradition by using the Moondala included after this chapter.

Wildschooling Moondala.

References

Holt, J. (1990). *Learning all the time: How small children learn to read, write, count, and investigate the world without being taught.* Da Capo Books.

Kimmerer, R.W. (2015). *Braiding sweetgrass: Indigenous wisdom, scientific knowledge and the teaching of plants.* Milkweed Editions.

7

The Journey of a Soulful Artist

Monet Poe

I imagine that given the choice, every child would choose freedom to be exactly who they came here to be. They would feel safe, loved, and free. They would choose to grow through play and exploration. They would choose to be seen and celebrated for their uniqueness. They would be free to grow without expectations, grades and levels, and all the boxes and labels that humans have created. They would choose to be wild and free. At least, that's what I chose. I didn't come to Earth to fit into any boxes. I came to be me!

DOI: 10.4324/9781003267362-8

I can't introduce myself without telling you about my mom first, because she is the reason I am who I am today. It's always been me and my mom, two peas in a pod. My parents got divorced when I was young, but I don't remember any of it, because I was two. Sarah is my mom and my teacher. She has always been such a kind person. She has a big heart. I have so many memories of us being silly and always making the most of whatever experiences life gave us. There were many things that my mom wanted to protect me from, so she did her best to protect me and give me the freedom to grow naturally and express myself authentically. She is my cheerleader and my partner in business too. Together we are sharing our hearts to help other families and children on their unique journeys, whether they choose to homeschool or not. We believe every child is born unique and they are here to share their gifts.

I'm a spiritual purpose coach for youth, an artist, a watercolor illustrator, and teacher and I believe in miracles and magic. I hope to inspire children to look in the mirror and see how beautiful and amazing they are. I hope to inspire parents to listen to their children and allow them to shine and show up authentically. I want to create a better world for free spirits and wild-hearted souls to flourish and share their magic.

Until I went to kindergarten, I was given all the freedom, love, and support to be my unique, creative, weird, and wonderful self. My mom and I spent a lot of time in nature; we played and we created. When I was born, my mom decided to leave her job as a music/art teacher to stay home with me. She opened a photography studio in our basement. From the very beginning, my mom and I were creating together. I'm very blessed that I had four fantastic grandparents as well. I spent a lot of my early years with them. We would cook together and play outside.

I was always a highly imaginative child, creating and dreaming a world of my own. I talked to fairies and angels and spent most of my time in nature. I would get an idea and my mom would give me the space and time to explore and create my ideas. She celebrated my creations and imaginations. She even came into my world with me. Together, we dreamed, created, talked to fairies, and made fairy houses. I had many "imaginary" friends and felt very strongly that my friend needed a car seat. My mom put two car seats in the car so that my friend "Charley" or "Spider man" (my imaginary boyfriend) could travel safely with me.

When I was four my mom decided she wanted to move us out of West Virginia, so she packed the car and set off to explore all the coastal towns on the east coast until one felt like home. We explored and found ourselves in Charleston, South Carolina, during an art festival. We fell in love and Mom went home, sold our house, and moved the two of us to Charleston a couple of months later. She wanted to give me opportunities to explore and experience the world in ways she wasn't given.

When I was five I was excited to go to school so my mom listened and found a small Montessori school on the beach for me. I have pretty fond memories of that year. I got to play and explore and wear tutus to school if I wanted. I have good memories of my teacher, Shannon, and I am still connected with her today. Shannon was there for me more than any other school I would experience in years to come.

I ended up going to a public elementary for first grade and that year was one of the hardest years for me. One day in first grade my mom decided to pick me up early for a big surprise; a Rusted Root concert! We love to see live music together and she loves to surprise me! On this day, she was the one who was surprised to find that I was not in the playground with the other students. Confused, she asked my teacher where I was. Her response was that I was in the library because I couldn't finish my schoolwork on time in class. Isolated in the library, I had been punished and assigned to complete my assignments in lieu of recess.

Needless to say, my mom was both furious and heartbroken. Children shouldn't be punished for how fast or slow they complete their work. That was one of the pivotal moments that gave my mom the courage to pull me out of school.

I have a lot of painful memories from those few years in the school system. Three different schools and the same patterns repeated. I experienced so much struggle. I may not remember specifics, but what I remember most is the feelings that I felt, because sometimes those feelings still surface even today. I felt ashamed. I felt stupid. I felt less than other children. I felt small. I started to worry more.

By the end of first grade, my teachers and principal had labeled me as ADHD. A few years later I would be diagnosed with dyslexia, dyscalculia, and APD (auditory processing disorder). They told my mom and I that I would never be able to focus or sit still. They went as far as telling my mom that I would never be able to succeed without medication and special classes. They also said that without medication I would stay in the lowest percentile of the class. Adderall for a six-year-old? I'm so grateful that Mom stood up for me even when teachers, friends, and principals told her over and over that she was failing me.

My mom listened, respected, and stood up for me. She had similar experiences in school and her own life and she wasn't going to let those things happen to me. She was going to change things for me and our family!

A child is imprinted in the first seven years of its life by how they have seen and experienced the world. Patterns of beliefs, feelings of safety, worth, value, fears—a child's first seven years of life play an important role in spiritual intelligence. Humans operate in seven-year cycles; even a majority of our cells are replaced every seven years. If a child is given a safe, nurturing environment to be seen, heard, and loved for exactly who they are, they are likely to develop a strong sense of security and self-worth.

Imagine if children were given the freedom to simply play, explore, and enjoy nature and healthy, loving relationships in those first seven years. What a different world we'd live in. No pressure to pick the right preschool or compare reading abilities or math skills. Instead, children would play and connect with nature, cook with parents, listen to stories from elders, sing songs, make art, and develop a loving relationship with themselves and, in tandem, with the world around them. It's a dream that my mom and I share, and why we do what we do in the world now. I had these opportunities, but not through formal education.

In my elementary school, I had many challenging experiences where the foundation of my worth was rocked. In first grade I had to write a book report and present it to the class. Being the creative child I was, I decided I would illustrate my book report. My teacher was not happy about it. She argued that I didn't do it like everyone else and gave me an F. Being a very passionate child as well, I stood in front of the class and said, "The illustrators are just as important as the authors and they don't always get the credit that they deserve." That did not go down well with my teacher.

Little did she know that I would grow up to become an illustrator and an art teacher. To this day, I still stand by that motto. There is so much more you can say in a painting than with words. You can feel the story on a deeper level then writing it out. I believe there is beauty in that. I wish I could go back to tell my teacher that there is more than one way to tell a story.

The public school was crushing my creative spirit inside me. I would come home from school sad and drained. I didn't want to be creative anymore. It felt as though they had stolen a part of me without my permission.

When we finally did choose homeschooling, I could learn in my own time and I was able to focus on the best way for me to learn. We used a variety of approaches—unschooling, Wildschooling, and nature schooling. My mom was the best teacher I could have asked for! She gave me the freedom to learn through play, joy, and curiosity. This has supported me in so many ways. She never graded any of my schoolwork and didn't even put me in a specific grade. Through that type of education, I continued to gained confidence in myself.

When I look back on my education as a child, I can remember how amazing it was to experience life through such a variety of learning environments. There were several internships which afforded me the opportunity to experience life lessons outside of the typical four walls in a public-school environment. I remember the struggles I had with reading, writing, and math and the overwhelming passion and patience my mom had with me. I'm so grateful for the path I chose. Sometimes I think about what my life would be like if I had stayed in the school system. All I can say is that I would probably be a different person than the one I am today. I don't know if I would be on the same life path.

Unschooling gave me the opportunity to take apprentice-ships, study what I was interested in, and take unique classes. I took pottery, swing dance classes, and worked alongside my mom on photo shoots. One of my favorite experiences was the apprenticeships at horse farms where I learned how to manage the daily routine of the barn and received hands-on learning experience with all the various horses. The seed for a future dream started growing when I started connecting with horses on a deeper level. This is a part of the gift of homeschooling.

The freedom to grow and explore at my own pace allowed me to have authentic learning experiences and to learn life lessons in the real world. I wasn't sitting at a desk in school studying science and the Earth's gravity. I was at the beach or in nature learning these concepts and lessons first-hand; watching the waves come crashing down or watching the acorns and the leaves fall from the trees. But, most of all, I was learning through the joy of play. I was learning and I was having fun. Do you know that humans learn best through play? Yes! We learn best through play and we retain what we learn when we are learning through the frequency of play and joy!

If you were homeschooled, you have probably heard; "Oh, you're homeschooled! How do you make friends? How are your social skills?" Society tell us that if you are homeschooled, you must be awkward, shy, weird, and struggle with relationships. It's quite a big myth that homeschooled or unschooled children have terrible social skills because we must "live under a rock" or are "sheltered." That is not true at all. Just because homeschool-ers don't go to a public school does not mean we don't have social skills. In fact, we are more likely to develop deeper rela-tional skills and not be conditioned through peer pressure. We understand who *we* are and discover *our* passions.

When you are homeschooled, you learn to ask questions and become much more independent. I also attended another home-school group growing up which allowed us to play in the woods. It was through these lessons where we learned cooperation and communication skills. The majority of my friends were either other homeschoolers or adults. I was very sociable as a child so it was easy for me to develop friendships wherever I was. In my opinion, social skills aren't linked to school. Human beings have been relating to one another from the beginning of time. How we relate and connect to humans is determined by other factors. There are plenty of opportunities for children to interact with other children and develop skills like communication, listening, sharing, cooperation, and co-creation. I attended homeschool groups and explored the world with my mom which encouraged a strong independence and a feeling of safety in the world. I believe I can go anywhere in the world and make friends. Even if there are language differences, we can connect with others on so many levels. Why? Because it is all about our frequency; the frequency of love and harmony.

I found that adults became easier to talk to more so than children my own age, but I believe this has more to do with my unique soul. I've been called an "old soul with a youthful spirit." I enjoy conversations with adults and yet I love to play and I'm still curious about the world. I also had dreams to start businesses and do things that society calls "grown up" from an early age. Why is it that children are supposed to condense learning into twelve grades and college? Isn't this industrial revolution concept outdated? Why aren't children supported to create businesses or do what they are here to do from an early age?

My experience of being given the freedom to learn and develop on my own terms, in my own time, at my own pace, has made me who I am today. I started my first business when I was ten, selling art at farmer's markets. Then, my mom and I had a dream to create an organic farmer's market with live music, kids activities, and community outreach. So we did. Together we created a beautiful farmer's market when I was 13. My mom put me in charge of booking bands and running the children's booth. This helped me learn responsibility and showed me what I was capable of creating. Every week I produced a new activity for the children and we had a blast!

Traveling has also been one of my greatest teachers. I love to travel. Exploring nature, culture, and learning the history of a place first-hand and meeting people from around the world is both inspiring and expansive. My mom and I had planned to take a trip to volunteer somewhere in the world when I was 16.

We had talked about working at an orphanage or building houses somewhere. Our spirit guides were listening and preparing, or more likely, it was always part of our souls' plan. In 2016, my mom and I were called to Standing Rock.

In September 2016, water protectors were already gathering by the Cannonball River on the Standing Reservation in North Dakota. The Dakota Access Pipeline was scheduled to run through the reservation via a native burial ground. This risked contamination of the waterways on the reservation. A group of Lakota youth had made a stand earlier in the summer to stop the pipeline and, soon after, their parents, aunties, uncles, and unci's joined them. The call went out and thousands listened, including me and my mom.

My mom and I woke up one morning, both with tears running down our cheeks. We both had the same dream the previous night, a dream that was calling us to go to Standing Rock. And we listened. It took us two days of driving all day and night in a caravan with some friends to get there. The families that went with us were also homeschooled and we would meet many more from around the world who also followed their wild hearts to be a part of this movement.

When we arrived it felt like a place we knew already. We set up camp, started making friends, and found ways to help.

The children who were wildschooled definitely knew how to jump in and help! We were a group of wild, nature-loving youth who knew how to create shelter, build fires, cook food, use a knife, and more importantly, how to listen, make conversations, and offer a helping hand.

A few days into our trip that was meant to be for two weeks, we knew. My mom and I lay in our tent, listening to the drums, crying buckets of tears. We were home. We let our friends know that we didn't want to go back to Charleston with them. Seeing that winter was on its way and all we had were some light Charleston weather jackets, we made the wise choice to drive back to Charleston and prepare more. Weeks later we returned to Standing Rock prepared to stay for as long as the spirit led. And we did.

Those seven months at Standing Rock changed my life, my mom's life, and many others' lives forever. I learned more about myself and the world. I made friends from around the world. I got to sit in circles with elders, medicine women and men, and people from all different cultures. I was welcomed into the Indigenous Youth Council. I learned more in those seven months than I could put into words. It's simply feeling. This is the opportunity that my mom has given me; to follow my spirit where it leads and to let my life be an unfolding journey trusting that my soul knows what is best for me.

Standing Rock showed me what was possible when we come together in a good way. I fell deeper in love with nature and, most importantly, I gained a strong sense of my place in this world and how I want to show up authentically in love and service for the highest good. Since then, we continue to spend time in the Dakotas supporting amazing Indigenous-led creations on Pine Ridge, Rosebud, and Standing Rock. Our hearts have forever been changed by the love we feel for the Oyate, the youth, and the land.

We are all born to be wild and free. We are all divine beings and we come to Earth with purpose and gifts that are unique to us. We are not created to fit into boxes, to learn the same way, or to follow the same path. We are born to create from our own unique hearts. This is the gift of being homeschooled. I'm using my experiences, combined with my soul's gifts and my heart, to support youth, young adults, and families now. No, I didn't go to college. I've followed my intuition and my passions.

Several years ago I developed an interest in human design and the gene keys after my mom started studying them. I'd always loved astrology and the stars and I've been passionate about inspiring children to follow their dreams and trust their intuition. I love to inspire soul purpose in others. Instead of asking a child, "What do you want to BE when you grow up?" you could simply ask a child, "What do you love to do? What are you passionate about? What do you want to experience?" The truth is that every one of us came to Earth with passions and purpose, and we get conditioned out of who we are when our parents, teachers, or society try to tell us who we should be or who they expect us to be.

I want children to be celebrated for exactly who they are. I want parents to see children as soul beings, just like them. I want children to be given the freedom to be who they came here to be.

So now I support youth and families to understand who they are, how their energy works, what their unique gifts are and how to support each other. There are too many children in the world who are suffering in school because its overwhelming environment doesn't support them; it causes more harm than good.

I don't have ADHD. I am empathic, intuitive, creative, and sensitive. I work best when I get the sleep I need. I work best in an environment that I create. I am sensitive to light, sound, touch, foods, and the energy of others. If you'd like to go by my diagnosis and say I have ADHD, go right ahead, but I'm not here to put myself in a box for others. I am here to shine my unique light in the world and to inspire others to do the same.

I can say that I am grateful for all my experiences that have led me to today, because every experience shapes us. It is up to us to choose *how* it shapes us. Because of everything I went through and what I've learned, I chose to support children and families.

My mom and I co-created Family Alchemy together last year. We combine human design, astrology, gene keys, and other tools to help families understand each other on a soul level. These systems have been very helpful for me and mom, so now we share them with others. Most children who are diagnosed with one of the "letter labels" like ADHD are actually highly intuitive and empathic, or their energy flows in a unique way. It would be a pretty boring world if everyone worked the same way. Since we are all energetic beings, it is important to understand how your unique energy works; some people have bursts of energy to create and then their bodies need to rest. Others have so much energy that they are great at multitasking and need to move their bodies a lot to release energy in a good way. Knowing ourselves is key to understanding and supporting each other.

Magic is the art of doing nothing outside your own divine nature. This is the heart of what Mom and I share with the world! You are magic. You are divine. You are a living miracle here to share your special brand of awesome. No labels required.

8

Weaving Unschooling and Forest Schooling in Australia

How it Works for Our Families

Nicki Farrell & Vicci Oliver

What Is Forest School?

For us at Wildlings, our own business we co-founded, Forest School provides the time, outdoor space, resources, and mentors to undertake hands-on, child-led, and often risky or adventurous play in nature with friends. It's where learning happens naturally—in nature. It really is that simple and simultaneously complex; that wholesome and beautiful. In traditional settings it is often described as a regular outdoor nature-based program that focuses on the holistic development of the child. We really love that because there aren't many philosophies that openly state that they're focusing on holistic development. Children engage in hands-on learning with natural elements. They connect with nature and learn to safely take risks (Elliott & Chancellor, 2014).

Whilst the term has been modified and used to capture the attention of parents and guardians in some educational settings, the one thing that sets Forest Schooling apart from other forms of education is that it occurs outdoors, for extended periods of

DOI: 10.4324/9781003267362-9

time, regularly. A huge part of the Forest School philosophy, particularly for us at Wildlings, and here in Australia, is that Forest School occurs in all-weather with readily available risky play opportunities in spaces where children can direct their own play experiences. It's not just nature play—we actively encourage adventurous risk-taking and that is a really huge part of allowing children to build confidence, grit, resilience, and all of those really important life skills. Forest schooling alongside our children is a big part of designing the lifestyle that we want for our children and our families.

Our Own Children

Unschooling, or self-directed learning, is the most natural way in which humans learn. It can be hard to describe the process because the way in which one child learns is different to another, even within families. And so, there is no such thing as a typical day in the life of an unschooler. In our own families, we do have a flow or a rhythm to our weeks so that we can ensure that we balance our commitments, work, and play. We know that they're learning because we participate in a variety of offerings. Our children are exposed to a diverse spectrum of people within our community, learning from the young and old, most often on equal footing, with different types of activities most days of the week.

We have been starting our weeks with Adventure Monday, a social activity that takes us to magical wild spaces with our friends.

We work in the office on Tuesdays, so husbands and friends care for our children and do fun things with them.

Our children get dropped off at our Wildlings Homeschool Forest School program on a Wednesday afternoon (by choice, they don't have to go), while we work in the office.

They attend a full day co-op on Thursday with other children aged from three through to twelve where they experience a combination of the best parts of school, such as sports, performance, life skills, swimming lessons, and carnivals.

Each child will usually pick one other 'organized' activity that has sparked an interest. Over the years, this has ranged from piano to jujitsu and from hip-hop to soccer. They do a lot of reading, listen to audiobooks, and build Legos. They draw, paint, and play boardgames—all things 'schooled' kids do—just more of it. It's a pretty sweet life!

Working While Unschooling

We have a lot of flexibility in our lives. The early risers get to wake early; unless we have a commitment, we can sleep in. We like to remind ourselves that kids are humans too. Sometimes, just like us, they wake up on the wrong side of the bed and might need a quiet day and it's not a big deal. They're not going to miss a test or assessment by missing a day at co-op or Forest School.

Whilst we may not sit down and do math or English lessons, our children have many opportunities to learn literacy, numeracy, and STEM skills through meaningful life interactions.

The beauty of self-directed education, and homeschooling in general, is that we don't have to school our children while we work. We unschool, which means that we don't do formal lessons. That's not to say that they are not involved in structured learning opportunities of their choice. They may choose to do a formal workbook, or a structured online course or learning program. They choose to do it because they enjoy it or they want to learn more about a topic. Lessons are not penciled in a timetable, starting at 9 AM and finishing at 3 PM. Our children have reached those golden years where they are old enough to entertain—and educate—themselves.

It's not our life. It's not up to us to choose what we think they should be learning. They're their own sovereign beings. They think differently to us and they have different interests and talents to us. If we don't need to, why should we dictate what we think would be 'good' for them to learn? And what will that look like in 20 years' time anyway? Not even the education 'experts' can accurately predict that, only that future generations will need excellent people skills. To clarify a common misconception, letting children choose what they want to learn doesn't mean that our children are wild, crazy, ill-mannered layabouts. We still have to parent—they just get to choose what they learn because they get to follow their interests. All this is to say, our children 'learn' whilst they play, while we work.

Logistically, we have a supportive community and family around us that gives us the flexibility to commit to our work obligations. We have surrounded ourselves with people who can support us, share the care, and/or provide amazing opportunities for our children. We can't speak highly enough of our community and how they enrich our children's lives.

But the real answer to how we school while we work is that we've created our own business that allows for flexible hours. We've got an incredible team, which means we don't have to work full time, so our work suits our unschooling lifestyle.

Assessment

We don't feel the need to assess learning.

While many educators will argue that assessment is an important tool in educational programs, we would argue that it can actually be a barrier on the path of true learning. As soon as you decide to assess a child, one of many things can happen. The first is that children learn what it is they need to do in order to pass the assessment or achieve the desired result. And that may not be driven by desire to learn, but to please a parent or teacher or to avoid punishment or negative feedback. It also can send a message that the answer is important, not the process.

Second, children will work out the ways to hack the system, because that's what kids do well—they find shortcuts, so they can get their parents or their teachers off their back. So, you will be assessing them on their ability to play the game.

Children, particularly those the age that ours are at now, have no reason to be assessed in what they are learning. An 8-year-old's report card is going to have very little to no impact on their life outcomes. Particularly when you're homeschooling and you're working one on one, you don't need to assess them; you know if your child is struggling to make sense of words, concepts, or letters. We do women, in particular, such a disservice by whittling down and outsourcing what we intuitively already know.

We don't ask our children's pottery teacher to assess them on their coil pot. As adults, we would never join a pottery class where we were going to be assessed because as adults, we're not doing it for anyone but ourselves, for enjoyment, and because we want to learn a new skill. So why can't we let children do the same?

Parents may think they want a standard education for their child. But if their child doesn't fit that standard map, then assessment is going to negatively affect their child's self-worth and their ability to see beyond the grade on the paper.

Financial Considerations

When it comes to making major changes to accommodate homeschooling, regardless of philosophy, there are generally sacrifices that need to be made. From the beginning of our parenting journeys we made sacrifices on where we wanted to live, what cars we drove, and what holidays we went on, and we spent time working out ways to limit our spending. We then chose to build a business because we still felt the desire to be purposeful and contribute to our families financially. As our families grew we decided to move somewhere that would support our lifestyle and create opportunities that involve very little financial investment—like being in nature. There are mountains to hike, waterfalls to chase, rivers to float down, and stretches of beach to explore.

We created a business from the ground up. We designed it so that we could be outside with our children and with our community. We built exactly what it is that we needed to support this journey, and we now make an income from it. We have found purpose and a village.

Over time we have also learned that homeschooling doesn't need to be expensive. We have found ways to swap services, volunteer our time in exchange for discounted participation, and create a multitude of free events that enrich our weeks. We have organized a heap of events that we knew our children would love, and this often means our families get to participate for free.

Unschooling on the Road

Planning for trips, whether long or short, can be such a beautiful learning experience in itself. Combining geography, history, science, culture, the planning is half the fun. One thing that we both do well is being ok with the unexpected, so when things don't go to plan, we can problem solve or surrender to the moment. Rain, crowds, forgetting gear; all of these things can be overcome. We don't dwell on disappointment and curb our expectations.

We are able to take spontaneous trips, regularly, because of the flexibility that our lifestyle affords us. We are not bound by school holidays or weekends and can make the most out of off-peak periods. When you work for yourself, you can set up your team so they are not reliant on you being available. Empowering them to be problem solvers is the key. We have worked really hard to get the right people in our business so that we can step away and leave the business ticking along while we enjoy time on the road, or more accurately, in the forest or on the sea.

We have done enough trips now to know exactly what it is we need which, suffice to say, is not a lot. Our gear is packed and ready to go so that if nature beckons us, we can throw in some clothes and food and be on our way. Experience has taught us what foods work and what meals are easy to cook and clean.

Taking trips with our community is one of the reasons that we are able to go away so frequently. We camp with friends at least four times a year, and this can also take the burden out of being overly organized. When you've got 6–20 other families camping together, you will always find someone who can lend you a mallet so that you can secure your tent pegs or find a sliver of shade under a friend's shelter to shield you from the blaring sun because you couldn't fit in your car. That's the beauty of community.

Managing Household Duties

When it comes to household duties, managing your priorities is key. Sometimes things don't get done around the house because it would require sacrificing family time. Our attitude towards household duties is that it gets done when it gets done. That is also not to say that it is a pigsty; it's just not sparkling either. The washing may just have a home in the basket for days on end and we are okay with that.

Clutter and mess can be an issue when we want to be productive when working from home. Sometimes they're just the thing that we have to let go of in order to be able to meet everyone's needs. We each have little hacks that make life easier, such as making dinner that will last three nights. If one of our children doesn't like what is on offer then they can make themselves something else. We have taught them the life skills they need to meet their own needs and empowered them to make their own choices.

Our children are encouraged to help out with household duties where they can and where it's practical. So essentially, the family takes care of household duties. Our kids don't have chores, but they participate in keeping the house livable.

We've both spent a really long time rearranging, renovating, decluttering, and minimalizing 'stuff' in the house because the more things we had, the messier it got and the clutter caused tension in our parent/child relationships. It took some time to organize our homes to get them to the point where they finally feel like they're functional, employing systems to minimize the clutter.

Unschooling—The Right Choice for Our Families

When we chose to unschool there was a level of faith that we had made the right choice, and the most impactful moments have been watching our children learn to read. Other than social skills, mastering a level of literacy was a benchmark we wanted our children to meet, because literacy unlocks the world and opens your mind. However, we knew this had to happen in their own time and for reasons that were important to them—not on our arbitrary timeline.

We observed this developing through their thirst for knowledge, in the simple act of flipping through the Australian Bird Guide. Showing little interest in being taught to read, but asking enough questions about letters, the act of reading was developed by first observing some daily visitors to the house—magpies, honeyeaters, and noisy miners, and then referencing the book to find pictures. In the quest for more information, something just clicked. There was the realization that every bird had a name, and the process of reading just took off from there. As teachers, that was the 'holy shit' moment. What have we been doing our entire careers? What have we been taught? We were under the misguided idea that children *had* to be taught to read and spell or they would never read!

When we witnessed our children learning to read on their own, right in front of our eyes, with no coercion, we knew that life without school was not only possible; it was joyful, meaningful, and natural.

Drawbacks of Unschooling—Or Not?

We've tried really hard to be critical about this but we absolutely love educating our children this way because we are just living and learning alongside them. It feels natural, healthy, non-stressful, and often joyful.

We have fervent and strong beliefs in this philosophy.

Most of our challenges have little to do with homeschooling and would be present in our lives no matter our educational choices. Logistics, driving, the mental load of the to-do list; these are the things that cause us the most angst. This is where adopting a growth mindset has shifted our perspective. If we are struggling with something, what do we need to do to improve the situation? Do we need to communicate our needs clearly; do we need more support or a change in our daily rhythm? Even something like feeling frustrated at the amount of time spent traveling in the car (which is one distinct challenge when you can spend up to 40 minutes each way getting to where you want or need to go) can be reframed as a positive in our day. What is a positive moment from your ordinary days? For us, it can be that time in the car raging out to a song, enjoying the forest or ocean scenery, and being fully present. We might listen to an audiobook or our playlist of songs or a podcast, so that even driving time is valuable.

Any drawbacks are solvable. If you really hate homeschooling, you can go back to school. If you hate unschooling, you can go back to homeschooling. There's no end date to this. It's a journey.

Socialization

Our kids spend more time out with other people than they do at home with their families. We need to remember that homeschooling doesn't mean that you're at home, schooling. More often than not, we're 'not-at-home schooling.'

At school, children are segregated sometimes by gender and definitely always by age. In some of the schools we have taught at, children were even segregated at lunch. You can imagine the chaos that ensued with that. It's no wonder a lot of schools are having problems with a lack of prosocial behavior in the school yard at lunchtimes.

School is not a realistic portrayal of the real world. In no other place in the adult world are people segregated like that anymore, whereas unschooled children socialize with people of all genders and all ages all the time. They're generally very comfortable socializing with adults on an even par, which is not as common in school children because of the inherent power dynamic between adults and students. In general, unschoolers are very embedded in our communities. We know the butcher's name, we know the librarian's name, etc. We still participate in community soccer and all the things that school kids do as well, we just do more of it in the real world every day.

There is a vast array of parent mentors in our village at all these activities, with skills sets from felting to knot tying to jewelry making, coding to photography. There are musicians, song writers, graphic designers, builders, and business owners. Our children have access to these amazing, respectful, super talented mentors who are showing children that they don't just have to go to university to be successful and happy. There are other paths, other ways to get there. There's just such a breadth of contribution and no one's immune from it.

Another thing to point out is that, commonly, when teenagers aren't enjoying school or are having problems with bullying, the common advice is, "Don't worry, once you leave school you will find your people." Or, "Once you leave school, life will get easier." The question here is, if school is the be-all and end-all for socialization, why is this the advice we're giving young people? It's because school is often a place of pain for many people.

Outsider Observations

Our children are thriving in this lifestyle but the growth that we see is hard to compare because they have never been to school. Parents of school children often comment that our own children and the children that attend our Forest School are "very caring and inclusive," "respectful," and that there doesn't seem to be any "popularity politics." But the most common comment is, "Wow, your child has very good body awareness!"

Current research shows that over a quarter of Australian children are obese (Australia Bureau of Statistics, 2018). In the US, there are clear parallels with 22% of children obese in 2021 (Dyer, 2021). Furthermore, these children are more uncoordinated and have less core muscle strength (Hanscom, 2016). We don't see that at Forest School; we see the opposite. The children that attend are healthy, strong, and fit. We love seeing kids just being kids, and not having to sit down for six hours a day. We love watching them traverse over uneven ground and scale up the sides of waterfalls and be confident in their bodies because they have the opportunity to do that.

Nature equals health and happiness. And we know it's not such a simple equation. Life isn't that simple, there's inherent privilege in that premise. But when something is free and fairly accessible to most, why not use it if you can?

Our Children's Perspective

It's the only thing they know. They have nothing to compare it with. I know that they are very happy that we've made the decision that we've made. They're really aware that the world is sort of theirs and our little communities to explore. They see so many different groups of friends on a day-to-day basis and they really love that.

MASTER L (7 YEARS): It's fun. I feel free. I get to do all the things I want.
MISS E (9) YEARS: Being free. Some kids think we have to go to school so [they] think we're lying when we say we don't go to school.

It can be a moment in time that gives us some insight into how our children view their world. When we are on our way to an adventure on a perfect Bluebird day, we have heard comments like "Will those school kids get to go to the beach today?" Our heart breaks for those kids. It is our wish that they could go out and enjoy nature and be with their families and enjoy the world, even just a little bit more than they currently do.

✅ Do Something

- ◆ If you can't find what you're looking for, build it yourself!
- ◆ Don't get us wrong, we're glad they can read, but we're not checking curriculum boxes.
- ◆ Don't assume that you're going to find your village in the first term. It will take time to find your village within the homeschool village, and to find your village within each of the activities that you choose. Also, you can't rely on the village to see you two or three times and expect to have open arms and invitations to everywhere. You have to work at it, you have to ask for invitations and you have to show up, because there are so many people and activities, people can't invite everyone to everything. If you're waiting for people to invite you to places all the time, then you are going to find community hard. Don't be scared to say, "Hey, do you mind if I tag along?" All you can do is ask.

◆ In contradiction of the above, it's also valid for some groups to be exclusive. They might acknowledge that their group dynamics are great at the moment and that they'd love for you to join them later down the road, but not right now.

◆ There are a lot of teachers that have pulled their children out of school to homeschool/unschool and that's not simply because they're teachers and they feel they can teach them, it's because once they've had kids they have realized that perhaps it's not the best way for their child to learn, and that the school system is perhaps not the healthiest system for their children. Teachers are the canary in the coal mines—but no one's really listening.

◆ I think at some point we all wondered if we could do the whole homeschool thing, or if we would be failing our children. But, the answer is, you can.

◆ We strongly suggest going to visit a homeschool co-op or forest school and meeting some of the parents to see how much we all love it, how happy the children are, and how much freedom we have in our days.

◆ On the term: "school/schooling": we personally prefer the word educate to school, as we don't school our children. Our children choose how they wish to learn or educate themselves. And the way our children learn is simply by pursuing their interests and living their lives.

◆ It's not just a reframing of language (because language is important), it's an entire mindset change. Your child doesn't need to go to school to get an education to get what they need to live a happy and successful life. They will be educated and educate or learn all by themselves, simply by living.

◆ Our children have continuous adult modeling and emotional support in navigating social etiquette such as how to be a good friend, how to handle tricky, social situations, how to respond when things aren't going their way, how to have uncomfortable conversations. When we talk about our children looking after themselves, we are still around (as are many wonderful parents and other members of our unschooling village). In comparison, in schools, the role of the adult is one of authority, not a co-learner.

♦ We have spent a lot of time examining our own educational conditioning and what we have been raised to believe education and learning "should" look like, especially because we come from teaching backgrounds. We've had to examine and define what it looks like for our children. A question that we continue to ask about learning or content is—is it essential to live a happy and successful life and for our children to thrive? For our children to be active citizens and community members? We of course are still imparting our moral codes to our children and role modeling how to be supportive friends and making good decisions. In actual fact, it's likely they get more guidance in areas such as these that we feel are really important.

♦ We will say that social-emotional learning is really important to us. That's the main reason we homeschool. As high school teachers, we were witnessing the horrific mental health epidemic that is still currently ripping through our high schools. We realized we didn't want our teenagers trying to learn social-emotional skills from other teenagers who were also struggling with their social-emotional skills.

♦ We would say, "Give it time, give it time."

Simple ways to engage your baby's senses with nature

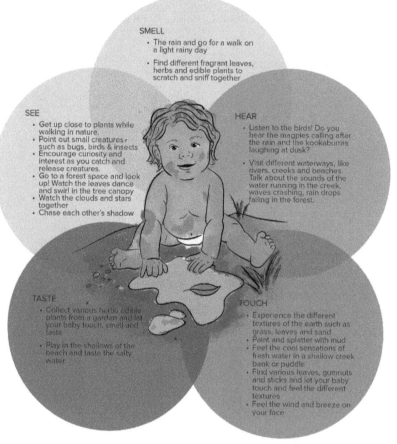

SMELL
- The rain and go for a walk on a light rainy day
- Find different fragrant leaves, herbs and edible plants to scratch and sniff together

SEE
- Get up close to plants while walking in nature,
- Point out small creatures such as bugs, birds & insects
- Encourage curiosity and interest as you catch and release creatures.
- Go to a forest space and look up! Watch the leaves dance and swirl in the tree canopy
- Watch the clouds and stars together
- Chase each other's shadow

HEAR
- Listen to the birds! Do you hear the magpies calling after the rain and the kookaburras laughing at dusk?
- Visit different waterways, like rivers, creeks and beaches. Talk about the sounds of the water running in the creek, waves crashing, rain drops falling in the forest.

TASTE
- Collect various herbs edible plants from a garden and let your baby touch, smell and taste
- Play in the shallows of the beach and taste the salty water

TOUCH
- Experience the different textures of the earth such as grass, leaves and sand
- Paint and splatter with mud
- Feel the cool sensations of fresh water in a shallow creek bank or puddle
- Find various leaves, gumnuts and sticks and let your baby touch and feel the different textures
- Feel the wind and breeze on your face

www.wildlingsforestschool.com

WILDLINGS
FOREST SCHOOL

RISKY PLAY PHRASES

As children continue to develop and test their physical boundaries, we must be mindful of the role our language plays in building their self awareness and resilience.

SIMPLE PHRASES TO USE INSTEAD OF "BE CAREFUL!"

- What is your plan?
- What can you use?
- How will you get down once you
- have reached the top?"
- What is your next move?
- Do you feel safe there?
- Take your time
- I'm here if you need me
- Do you feel stable/balanced?
- Do you need more space?
- Are you all still having fun?
- Can you make sure you can still see me?

SOME OPTIONS TO HELP THEM IF THEY GET STUCK OR RELUCTANT TO HELP THEMSELVES

- Try moving... your foot to that thick branch/your hand onto that rock
- Try using your... arms, feet, legs
- Can you reach that branch?
- Do you think your foot will reach that stone?
- Is there a way out/down from there?

HELPING KIDS MAKE OBSERVATIONS AND TUNE INTO THEIR SENSES

"Notice how the heat from the fire reaches me all the way back here? "

"Can you hear that rush of water? We need to keep an eye on those waves"

"Your friend is in your blood bubble. I'm worried that you might poke them in the eye with your stick. Can you please show your friend how to stay out of your blood bubble?"

"I can see a crack in that tree branch. Do you think it will hold your weight, or break?"

"Let's move this activity to an empty space to keep everyone safe"

"Can you see how sharp the knife is? It cuts through the carrot so easily. See how I only hold the knife by the handle? I never touch the shiny blade."

"You may need more space to play with that stick"

"Before you throw that rock, what do you need to look out for?"

USE YOUR OWN EXPERIENCES

"I remember when I slipped on the rocks when I was exploring the rockpools. Can you see the black algae there? It's so slippery!"

Create your own
Forest Fairy

Use some glue to stick on
leaves, bark, flowers and
other things you have
found in nature.

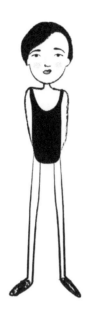

WEEKLY PROGRAMS HELPING CHILDREN TO
PLAY, EXPLORE AND FLOURISH IN NATURE.
www.wildlingsforestschool.com

WILDLINGS
FOREST SCHOOL

References

Australia Bureau of Statistics. (2018, 12 12). *Overweight and obesity*. Australian Bureau of Statistics. Retrieved 10 12 2021, from https://www.abs.gov.au/statistics/health/health-conditions-and-risks/overweight-and-obesity/latest-release

Dyer, O. (2021). Obesity in US children increased at an unprecedented rate during the pandemic. *BMJ, 374*(2332), Np.

Elliott, S., & Chancellor, B. (2014). From forest preschool to bush kinder: An inspirational approach to preschool provision in Australia. *Australasian Journal of Early Childhood, 39*(4), 45–53. doi: 10.1177/183693911403900407

Hanscom, A. (2016). *Balanced and barefoot: How unrestricted outdoor play makes for strong, confident, and capable children.* New Harbinger Publications.

9

A Balance of Screen Time and "Green Time"

An Interview with Linda McGurk

Katie Rybakova Mathews

According to the American Academy of Child and Adolescent Psychiatry (2020), children between the ages of eight and twelve spent, on average, four to six hours per day using or watching screens in 2020. For teens, this number grew to nine hours (AACAP, 2020). Among younger children, screen time exposure begins in infancy and often goes over the recommendations set forth by the American Academy of Pediatrics; no screens except for video chats for children up to 24 months and no more than an hour a day between the ages of two and five (Pappas, 2020). In an analysis of screen time in this age range between 1997 and 2014 in the U.S., Chen and Adler (2019) found the average screen time exposure for children two and under was a little over three hours a day, while 3–5-year-olds clocked in at about two and a half hours of screen time per day. Recent research found that healthy prekindergarten students that were exposed to screen time higher than the AAP recommendations suffered, "lower measures of myelination of brain white matter tracts and emergent literacy skills" (Hutton, Dudley, Horowitz-Kraus, Dewitt, &

DOI: 10.4324/9781003267362-10

Holland, 2020, p. 1), which then lead to subsequent lower cognitive assessments. Simply put, American children spend too much time in front of screens, and this is affecting them in a negative way. Caution with sweeping generalizations, of course, means that we have to recognize that screen time is an umbrella term used for a variety of activities using a number of products and platforms. An educational documentary that the entire family watches together and then discusses is different from the screen time exposure from watching an age-inappropriate film independently in one's room. Scholars like James Gee, for instance, point to what video games teach us about learning, in his aptly named book *What Video Games Have to Teach Us About Learning and Literacy* (2007). All in all, what we seek for our children is balance—enter what Linda McGurk, author of landmark book, *There Is No Such Thing as Bad Weather* (2017), calls a balance between "screen time and green time."

Nature-based learning—a broad term that encompasses "influences of experiences in nature on learning across the curriculum, personal development, and environment stewardship" among other delineations and nuances (Jordan & Chawla, 2019, para. 32), anecdotally seems to act as an antithesis of screen time, yet it does not necessarily have to be. Instead, a focus on nature-based learning, whether in the form of forest schools such as those depicted in McGurk's text, or as a homeschooler engaged in a variety of nature-based practices like the Charlotte Mason approach, or Wildschooling (Sowder, 2018), is simply a drive to experience life outside of the four walls of a classroom or home. Education in a nature-based environment has not had much focused empirical evidence, but recent research, such as Kuo, Barnes, and Jordan's (2019) work which focused on nature-based learning outcomes, shows the literature upholds positive developments in academic achievement, personal development, stewardship, and even individual concentration, stress levels, and engagement. Nature exposure, according to Kuo, Barnes, and Jordan (2019), varies from free play in nature to animal-assisted learning to camping experiences, with many other forms in between.

McGurk's book, *There Is No Such Thing as Bad Weather* (2017), accentuated her own experiences with nature-based education, particularly through the lens of cultural differences between Scandinavia and the United States. In the following interview, we discuss the benefits of nature-based education, the reality of screen time, and ways to encourage the entire family to head outside (regardless of the weather). The following interview was condensed and edited for clarity.

Katie Rybakova (KR): In your book, you talked about the Scandinavian way of life and how it is nature based. In your experiences, what is the outcome of this kind of education?

Linda McGurk (LM): *In Scandinavia, we have a forest school tradition. It is not homeschooling, but the education is grounded in a very nature-based curriculum. There are not only learning outcomes but also health benefits from this kind of curriculum. Research has found that children who have positive, direct experiences in nature together with people who are close to them usually have a stronger connection with nature later on in life and often end up being environmentally conscious as adults.*[1] *When children learn outside, all of their senses are activated, which helps learning tremendously. It is a holistic form of education that involves the whole child, and not just their academic performance. Outside, children are building excellent motor skills, strong bodies, and strong hands—those are the hands that will hold the pencils once they begin more traditional, academic work.*

Children play more creatively and more imaginatively outside. Anecdotally, I have found that children who go through this kind of education, as they get older, show a certain amount of grit. It is not something that I see as often in children who spent a lot of time inside. Children who spend a lot of time outdoors are comfortable in lots of different types of situations. This stems from being outside and being exposed to the elements. Through outdoor activities, such as climbing and cooking food outside, children learn to challenge themselves appropriately. They engage in risky play. This teaches risk management and promotes executive function, which is an important factor in success in later adulthood—more so than IQ and high grades. Resilience and grit foster executive function.

KR: Do you see a shift in how children play outdoors into adolescence? Is there a role for the parent?

LM: *Parents absolutely have a role in supporting their adolescents' outside activity. However, the older the children, the more limited your role as a parent becomes. In general, in the teenage years, children are more and more influenced by their peers and less by their parents. Children who have had a strong bond with nature from their young years have an advantage as they are firmly rooted in nature. They have that to fall back on. They might drift away from nature for a few years—I did when I was in my teens – but as a parent, you can still be there to support a nature connection and encourage family time outside. I try to do that with my children, who are 10 and 13 now. We keep our weekends fairly free so that we can do things as a family. The kids do not always want to go, but that time outside for us together is so important. It is also the parent's role to gradually give the child more and more freedom, which I talked about in my book. Freedom with responsibility! The older the child becomes, the more freedom you can give them. That will give them a chance to explore and to bond with nature in their own way. They might want to go camping with their friends on their own. As a parent you can support that.*

A lot of parents struggle with screen time. That is the reality of parenting today. A parent's role is to set limits and guide the healthy use of screens. Screens are not inherently good or bad. It simply depends on what you do with the devices. I am a big fan of balance. We have to find a balance between screen time and green time. If I am out with my children for a three-hour hike, I am fine with them sitting on their phones for a while, as long as they get that initial movement.

KR: How do home educators and alternative educators shift into a more nature-based approach when the child has become used to indoor and/or screen-based lifestyles?

LM: *Baby steps are crucial in shifting to a nature-based approach. When nature has not been part of a child's daily routine from the get-go, it usually takes more engagement from the adult. It may require the adult to be more "hands on" at the beginning to create that rhythm. It should not be a question of if we are going out today, but when. Gradually, make going outside a daily rhythm, even if you start by going out for just half an hour per day. Consider what makes your child excited and what they are interested in. Being flexible is important, but do not make it optional; for our family, it has always been an expectation to go outside every day.*

KR: Is there something parents can do to make an environment more conducive to this form of learning?

LM: *Nature-based environments needs to be accessible; the closer to home, the better. The backyard is an excellent place to start, especially with younger children. You do not necessarily want to manicure it too well either. The wilder the space, the more opportunities children have to play with materials. There are lots of different and creative ways to play, but if the space is already made up for them, the play will be a little less creative. There are many different features of a backyard that are really conducive to play. For instance, places to hide and climb, water, and an open space to run are ideal. Whatever you have access to though is a good place to create a space. A mud kitchen, for example, or even a big pile of dirt in your backyard, is a great play space. We built a house when my children were little and those piles of dirt that we had out there were the best toys. They played for hours in those dirt piles. We really do not need to overthink it. We should give children access to as many natural materials as possible and an environment with as much sensory experience as possible.*

KR: Is there a place for formal curriculum in a natural setting or does outdoor play serve an entirely different purpose?

LM: *There is definitely a purpose to a curriculum in a nature-based setting. We tend to automatically jump to ideas like worksheets or the alphabet when we think of curriculum, but a curriculum can be a lot of things. In the Swedish preschool, there is a national curriculum, but it paints with broad brushstrokes. The role of a curriculum in nature-based education can provide a framework but ultimately there is still a lot of creativity and free play. The educator provides the basics, but you still want education to be child-directed in this kind of education. The child and parent or teacher are co-discoverers. You discover things together. As children get older there could be a more formal curriculum like nature journaling but otherwise it is primarily hands-on learning. Any subject can be taught in nature in a developmentally appropriate way. We do get easily overzealous because we think we need to have all these activities—we feel like we need to structure classes or lessons. The foundation of nature-based education should be child-directed play with the teacher acting as co-discoverer.*

KR: Do you have any best practices or tips for home educators?

LM: *If children are going to be able to learn outside, they have to be comfortable. The basic needs need to be met. They need to be warm and dry; they need to have a full tummy; they need to have gone to the bathroom. Parents also need to be prepared, because inevitably they are going to get hungry, they might get wet, and they are definitely going to need to go to the bathroom at some point. It does take a bit of planning as to how to handle all that. It depends on your situation. Eating outside, for example, is an excellent way to start getting outdoors more. I know a lot of people are pressed for time—one simple tip to start getting outside more is do what you normally do inside, outside. Playdates and socializing with other people can be done outside. Make it a part of your life.*

I am a big fan of dressing for the weather and being outside in all seasons, because you want to be able to see the shifts in nature. We can see an alignment with seasons versus a regular calendar.

A lot of people, sadly, feel pressured by society to be very scheduled and have lots of activities. My advice would be to take a long and hard look at the calendar and see what you can do away with. Our children do not need to be nearly as booked up as they are. That is what is nice about being from Sweden myself— I have a cultural comparison to make. There is a different cultural standard. It can be very easy to get caught up in scheduling children for many activities and getting stressed about it. In Sweden we do something completely different, and the kids still turn out okay.

Note

1 See Chawla (2007) in references.

References

American Academy of Child and Adolescent Psychiatry. (2020). *Screen time and children*. Retrieved November 28, 2021, from https://www.aacap.org/AACAP/Families_and_Youth/Facts_for_Families/FFF-Guide/Children-And-Watching-TV-054.aspx

Chawla, L. (2007). Childhood experiences associated with care for the natural world: A theoretical framework for empirical results. *Children, Youth and Environments, 17*(4), 144–170.

Chen, W., & Adler, J. (2019). Assessment of screen exposure in young children, 1997 to 2014. *JAMA Pediatrics, 174*(4), 391–393.

Gee, J. (2007). *What video games have to teach us about learning and literacy*. St Martin's Griffin.

Hutton, J.S., Dudley, J., Horowitz-Kraus, T., Dewitt, T., & Holland, S.K. (2020). Associations between screen-based media use and brain white mater integrity in preschool-aged children. *JAMA Pediatrics, 174*(1), 1–10.

Jordan, C., & Chawla, L. (2019). A coordinated research agenda for nature-based learning. *Frontiers in Psychology, 10*(766), 1–10.

Kuo, M., Barnes, M., & Jordan, C. (2019). Do experiences with nature promote learning? Converging evidence of a cause-and-effect relationship. *Frontiers in Psychology, 10*(305), 1–9.

McGurk, L. (2017). *There's no such thing as bad weather: A Scandinavian mom's secret for raising healthy, resilient, and confident kids*. Touchstone.

Pappas, S. (2020). What do we really know about kids and screens? *American Psychological Association, 51*(3), 42.

Sowder, N. (2018). Wilder child. Retrieved July 25, 2021, from https://wilderchild.com/about/

Interlude

Shared Lessons for Democracy?

Robert Kunzman

These are troubled times for our political systems and public squares.

Historians will argue that this observation has applied to many times and places, and no doubt they are correct. But clearly these days are filled with great strife among citizens and profound disputes about the proper shape of our public life together.

Why raise this topic in a book about modern homeschooling? I think it poses a critical question about the education of our youth: how should we prepare them for the rights and responsibilities of democratic citizenship?

As the contributors to this book are well aware, one of the great advantages of homeschooling is the flexibility it provides children and adolescents to engage in learning experiences that match their needs and interests. I want to suggest, however, that the shape of a young person's education should not be guided solely by these individual variables.

Democracy depends on the cultivation of certain civic values in its citizens. This doesn't mean agreements about tax structures, immigration policies, or environmental regulation, but rather shared commitments about how we will engage with one another amidst our inevitable disagreements, and an appreciation for the political processes that enable us to make decisions about our shared life together.

DOI: 10.4324/9781003267362-11

Part of the reason that civic conflict and disagreement are so pronounced is that we live in societies marked by deep value pluralism—our priorities and visions for a "good society" cannot always be reconciled. Instead, we need to figure out how to live together *despite* those differences, in ways that still keep us committed to one another in some fundamental way.

One commonly cited civic virtue is that of political tolerance—the willingness to extend civil liberties to those with whom we disagree (and perhaps even dislike). But that's not enough. We need to know enough about our neighbors—near and far—to appreciate *what matters to them and why*. Political tolerance alone does not require us to step outside of our own echo chambers.

Of course, we will not always feel warmly toward our fellow citizens and their priorities, and familiarity doesn't always breed affection; sometimes, the better we know someone, the more we *dislike* them. But my point here is not about emotional affection, but rather what political theorists term "civic friendship"—a sense of mutual identification that includes the recognition that we need to be mindful of what our fellow citizens care about, and that we need to be willing to exercise the twin virtues of compromise and accommodation.

Compromise requires us to know enough about others' unfamiliar perspectives to appreciate possibilities for common ground—or at least appreciate the significance of what others are giving up when they compromise with us. But sometimes common ground will not be found, and here we need to seek accommodation, which involves finding ways to recognize and honor what matters to our fellow citizens with whom we disagree. Efforts toward accommodation depend on civic friendship—a commitment to keep talking, keep listening, and recognize that we shouldn't get everything we want and sometimes we need to give ground, even when the vote tally doesn't require it and self-interest doesn't advise it.

This is fundamentally a relational vision of citizenship—not of affection, but of mutual obligation. Civic friendship across cultural, ethical, and political differences is not necessarily a natural act. We often prefer the company of like-minded people. With this in mind, it seems critical—no matter the form of education—

to provide opportunities for young people to cultivate relational ties with people who are outside of one's own tribe, transcending typical social boundaries shaped by race, class, and religion.

How can we prepare young people for this kind of citizenship? Research on homeschoolers' civic development has been inconclusive, in large part due to inconsistent data collection and small sample sizes. But we do know a fair bit about civic development in students more generally. While my emphasis here is more on civic values than content knowledge, we find that young people who know more about their government are more likely to vote, discuss politics, contact the government, and take part in other civic activities than their less knowledgeable counterparts.

Some research also finds that certain kinds of school curricula positively influence students' intentions to become civically involved as adults. The strongest effects emerge from service-learning opportunities and engaging with problems in the community, combined with opportunities for students to have open dialogue about controversial topics important to them. We know that participation in voluntary groups focused on community service, public speaking, and fostering communal identity all appear to make future political engagement more likely.

Parents serve not only as important models for civic volunteerism but also as dialogical partners: adolescents who talk about politics with their parents score higher on measures of civic skills and behavior. It's interesting to note that parents and adolescents don't need to have similar viewpoints in order for teens to cultivate a commitment to democratic citizenship—what is vital, however, is that parents model a dialogical process whereby they genuinely listen to their children's perspectives, and they create space for their kids to hold their own opinions on issues. Political talk at home is important in cultivating civic awareness and involvement, but it cannot simply be an echo chamber where alternative perspectives are merely caricatured.

For philosopher of education John Dewey, the proper goal of education was growth. Toward what end? More growth. This open-ended approach sounds like a good fit with unschooling. But Dewey also emphasized the need for young people to learn how to be democratic citizens—not by studying it, but by engaging in it as a mode of associated living, by living it out as part of their group learning experiences. This may require some intentionality, but it can still fit comfortably within an education that is open-ended and student-directed. To the extent that democracy depends on citizens committed to its ongoing cultivation and renewal, this seems a goal worth pursuing, no matter the form of education we choose.

10

Trust in Your Journey

Lessons from a Worldschooling Family

George Kaponay

There are two stories which encompass some of the greatest challenges, obstacles, joys, and turning points we have faced in our lives over the past 12 years as a family. Along with my wife Bobi and our twins Réka and Lalika, these experiences taught us to *always trust* in our journey of learning together. They taught us that a homeschooling, unschooling, or worldschooling journey is much less about the content you choose to learn along the way, and much more about the adventure you choose to embark on as a family.

Our own family adventure has seen us sell our house and most of our belongings, go from working high pressure 80-hour weeks, to starting a non-profit project which evolved into the business we run together as a family today, to traveling the entire spectrum of what learning could look like for us, and ultimately, live, experience, and appreciate the people, places, and cultures of 52 countries on six continents.

Along this adventure, we discovered that consciously choosing to listen to and empower each other equally as full stakeholders in our family enabled us to take sovereignty over the way in which we lived our lives. This choice made it easy

DOI: 10.4324/9781003267362-12

for us to listen to our hearts, follow our intuition, trust in our choices, and stick to our convictions in the face of many dissenting and judgmental voices.

One of the most picturesque hikes we did on a beautiful autumn afternoon just outside of Ouray, Colorado, USA.

Listen to Your Intuition

In late 2013, we were standing at a significant crossroad as a family. We had been traveling for 18 months non-stop through North and South America, and now found ourselves looking for a place to slow down and rest for a little longer term. This would save on expenses, as well as provide us with a very necessary respite from constantly traveling from place to place which, while fun initially, had very quickly become quite draining.

At the time, we were traveling with Mark and Susie (pseudonyms), an older couple from the U.S. whom we had met while traveling in Ecuador in 2012. Nine months after our meeting, they contacted us out of the blue, telling us they wanted to relocate from Ecuador to Europe, seeking our assistance. Though their contact was somewhat unexpected, it seemed fortuitous, as we were struggling to see the purpose of remaining in North

America. It was draining our limited funds and our non-profit project *EnergeticXChange* had not gained the traction we were hoping for in the U.S. Susie also apparently had European heritage through her grandfather, and they proposed it as a business opportunity for us to help them to relocate.

Five weeks after this initial conversation, we found ourselves in Morocco, ready to do a little exploring while working out the finer details and next steps. Things had been exciting when we were discussing the prospect of linking our journey together for a time in our Skype calls, but when we met Mark and Susie in Marrakesh, somehow the reality of things were different. They didn't have the same light-hearted disposition; something was troubling them. We all felt it, our children especially. But whatever it was, instead of addressing it, we put it to the back of our minds.

Mark was in constant pain from what he described as chronic physical ailments related to his long-term scoliosis. As they had never had children before, by early afternoon, right around the time his daily regimen of painkillers was starting to wear off, he was often irritated by our children.

As those initial days passed and we explored Marrakesh together, we learnt for the first time that Mark and Susie had once been long-term, higher up members of a well-known meditation cult. They didn't exactly give a full explanation as to why but admitted that it was one of the reasons they had to leave the U.S. a few years earlier. A few days later, they told us that they wanted to choose new names for themselves. They also insisted we call them Aunty and Uncle. So right then and there, Mark and Susie became Uncle John and Aunty Nelly. Major red flag? Perhaps, but understanding what it was like to be misunderstood, we gave them the benefit of the doubt and looked instead toward how we could integrate our plans to work for everyone.

As we entered the second week of traveling together, while visiting the Berber people of the Atlas Mountains, John continued having bouts of incoherence due to his heavily opiate induced states. He constantly exhibited a dissatisfaction over what he expressed was our decision to visit and explore Morocco before going to Europe. He kept insisting this was a mistake, feeling that "the optimal plan" was to head immediately to Europe, even though it was John and Nelly themselves who'd insisted we should meet in Morocco when our initial European accommodations had fallen through. At the time of booking, we had even presented several more cost-effective options for them and us to arrive and meet in Europe, all of which they'd immediately rejected. They were explicit in requesting their flights not transit through a specific list of countries. We didn't ask why at the time; however, we would later come to realize that these countries all had extradition treaties with the U.S.

On day ten of our trip, we realized we were going to be a mere 1-hour ferry and 2-hour bus ride away from a good friend in Spain whom we had never met in person. Subsequently, when we let our friend Kingsley know, he immediately extended an invitation for all of us to come visit and stay with him for the weekend. But when we discussed this opportunity with Uncle John and Aunty Nelly, we encountered quite the wall of opposition. Immediately, the mood of our train carriage shifted from light-heartedness to one of tenseness and quiet.

We had discussed this as a family and almost in unison, we'd expressed how we were all starting to feel the strain of the energy from John, constantly wanting to control or even manipulate situations. In listening to our intuition, we decided it was vital for us to travel to Spain.

When we reached our accommodation in Asilah, we spent the afternoon with Nelly organizing and paying for our final two flights to our European destination together. When we asked Nelly about John's feelings, she dismissed it, saying it was just the pain talking. At dinner, we, but especially our daughter Réka, explained to them why we had such a strong intuitive feeling that we had to make this journey to Spain. They told us that they understood, but also, that they wouldn't be coming with us. Instead, they assured us that they would be waiting in Asilah for our return on Monday afternoon, and that on Tuesday morning we would fly out to Europe, just as we had planned.

As it turned out, they were neither waiting for us, nor did they end up coming to Europe at all. When we returned, we found a completely empty apartment. We would learn from our Moroccan hosts that John and Nelly had left our shared accommodations in the dead of the night. We later learned, through an email, that they had booked and paid for flights to Nepal, insisting John needed immediate attention at a special Ayurvedic spinal clinic, and we have never seen them since.

For us, meeting our friend across the Moroccan waters in Andalusia not only inspired us to live in Spain, (which we did, starting in 2014 for nearly 2 years), but for our daughter, it was a momentous experience. That one weekend set in motion a direction and course that completely changed her life.

For it was in Andalusia, close to the stroke of midnight, not wanting to go to sleep and sneaking around in the hallway listening in to our conversation, that she met another member of the household. Himself a budding teenager, sneakily sauntering back into the house after a night-time adventure with his friends, it was Fuko, the young Patterdale Terrier *dog*, who as she herself says, chose her to reveal his secrets, and created the instance which inspired her to write her debut fantasy-adventure novel, *Dawn of the Guardian*. This was published two years later when she was just 14, making her one of the world's youngest published authors. This one encounter was also the spark that launched us on an 18-month global book tour, that saw us engage in over 100 live events with schools, libraries, bookstores, home-ed learning groups, worldschooling communities, conventions, and even two TEDx Talks, throughout which, countless new, meaningful, and inspiring connections and friendships were made.

Had we given in to the pressures of John and Nelly, I have come to feel that our lives would have taken a very different course. But in trusting our inner voice of intuition, we reaped the benefit of knowing ourselves, individually and as a family, ever so much more intimately.

And so, I have come to understand that no matter how uncertain or outlandish the wild world becomes where you roam, being in the moment, flowing like water, and trusting yourself enough to listen to *and act on* your intuition, will always return you to your axis and guide you forwards to your true north with the inner compass we all possess.

In the Peruvian desert at the mystical Nazca Lines, an incredible learning experience for us all in archeology, geology, and the esoteric!

There are Times the Only Transportation Available Is a Leap of Faith

It was 2012, and less than a year into our worldschooling journey, we were reaching the end of an epic 6-month saga of traveling through South America, living in and exploring Colombia, Ecuador, Peru, Chile, Argentina, Paraguay, and finally, Brazil. We had achieved this on less than a shoestring budget of US$5,000, and this had even enabled us to live some particularly mind-blowing experiences, especially in Peru where we were invited to spend a week at *Communidad Keros*, a small village where *the living descendants of the Incas* spent their summer days shepherding their herds at an altitude of 4,500 m [14,764 ft] by the sacred Apu Wasi of the Andes Mountains. This was a community that at the time no other foreigners had visited, except for one previously invited National Geographic photographer from Japan.

On the last leg of this 6-month journey, we reached Rio de Janeiro, but only just. We had made a critical budgeting error when planning our visit to Iguazu Falls. The 42-hour bus journey from Cordoba, Argentina to Iguazu had cost us less than US$200 and we made the rookie error of assuming that it would be at least half the price from Iguazu to Rio, because it was half the distance. Standing at the bus station to book our tickets to Rio, we thought they had made a calculation error, shocked to learn it would cost over US$900.

The problem was that at that moment, we had less than US$400 in total. This was meant to sustain us over the week in which we wanted to take in the sights of Rio, over our last day in Bogota, Colombia, and on a final layover in Panama which would ultimately return us to the U.S.

To add to this strain, we'd just had a rather hair-raising incident the night before in Iguazu's town center. Our son Lalika, by complete accident, bumped into a very expensive crystal sculpture in a shop, shattering it while we were browsing. This piece was over US$800 in value, and we were made to wait for the shop owner to come. When I explained to him in all sincerity that I literally had less than $400 in total to my name and seeing the absolute horror and concern in my eyes, the shop owner, with the greatest of humanity simply said, "Don't worry about it." This was another moment of many along our journey that very personally illustrated to us the inherent generosity of all human beings.

The truth is though, that it was only because of our son Lalika that we were able to travel throughout South America, having the breadth and depth of learning experiences that we did on such a meager budget. Through his passion and dogged determination to follow through, he demonstrated an almost superhuman ability at utilizing research and the Internet to find us the most cost-effective modes of travel.

He had found and introduced us to all the emerging short-term accommodation websites, bearing in mind that it was early 2013, he was only 11 years old, and these services were all in their infancy, unknown by the masses. These alternatives saved us hundreds of dollars and delivered us from the overpriced, bedbug ridden hotels we had stayed in earlier in our journey.

He also found and expertly navigated cheap aggregator flight websites, nearly all of which had just started operations the year before. Impressively, he even figured a way in which when we used a local VPN to buy the tickets directly from the airline's website, we got served discounted local prices, instead of the inflated prices algorithmically reserved for those in the U.S. This meant a minimum difference of between US$150–250 per ticket, on already discounted flights, which on average saved us sometimes upwards of US$800–1,000 when we traveled by air.

In relation to our very real predicament in Iguazu, he took us by complete surprise when, he said to me, "Dad I think I've solved this. I've found us flights for US$140 from Iguazu to Rio, via São Paulo." *US$140 in total for all four of us,* or US$35 a ticket.

Although we had to spend the night at the Iguazu airport terminal, our flight to Rio was a mere four hours, and by early the next day, we were relaxing in an excellent 3-star private hotel accommodation Lalika had found us, in a great neighborhood for just $32 a night.

This meant we still had enough money for food, public transport, and potentially all the attractions for which Rio is famous. And yes, we visited Ipanema and the Cristo Redentor, but it was the more unsung experience that would always define Rio de Janeiro for us as a family.

Wherever we stay, we always like to walk and explore the surrounding neighborhoods and, if possible, get to know the stories of the local people. It was on our fourth day in Rio, with the equivalent of US$40 of Brazilian reals in our pocket, that we wandered up to a large sign at the bottom of a very steeply ascending hill. The sign had *Santa Marta* written on it. We found ourselves intermingling with a diverse group of people, among them a tour group of elderly U.S. citizens. Circling them were "neighborhood ambassadors" who were organizing a tour for this group to visit a real *favela*.

Real, in-fact, was not at all an exaggeration of the truth. In 2013, Santa Marta, as a community, was still experiencing drug-related organized crime violence. The community had done much since 2010 to create a program that would eventually succeed in ending criminal activity, however, at this time, outsiders were still only being taken up to the community by these neighborhood ambassadors. We heard one of the ambassadors speaking with the U.S. tour group and approached him inquiring about the cost. He offered to take us up for US$100 per person, eventually dropping his price to US$70. When we truthfully explained our monetary situation, his welcoming smile immediately turned cold as he started to walk away. We asked whether it was forbidden for outsiders to go up, his answer was, "If you wish to risk your family's life, go ahead, we will take no responsibility."

It is without exception that wherever we have traveled, if there is a consciously organized effort to improve the community, and if it is culturally appropriate, respectful, and possible to contribute, whether monetarily or with an in-kind contribution of work or assistance, we will always opt to do so. In this case, we had offered the ambassador the US$20 we were carrying which, in retrospect and deference to him, he could not have known, was literally half of what we were monetarily worth at the time. Looking at us through an assumptive lens, which we unfortunately choose to take as humans because it is easier to do so, especially with first appearances, he must have felt that we were being disrespectful to him and the neighborhood. This was certainly not our intention, but that bit of what Australians like to call *the mongrel* in us, that rears its head especially when people choose to try to scare us, was activated, and we felt an obvious, audacious desire to prove that the world isn't half as dangerous as what people make it out to be. "Let's go!" we exclaimed in unison, and with that we ascended the steep hill into the heart of the neighborhood.

What we experienced that day was not assault, nor getting robbed, nor being left for dead. Instead, we met a vibrant community of people who, like all people across the globe, are trying their best, the best way they know how, to make their way in this world.

In choosing to open ourselves without fear to whatever Santa Marta had to offer and what we had to offer it, we had a completely different experience to the ones normally and negatively highlighted in the media. Everyone we passed greeted us with a welcoming good afternoon in Portuguese, to which we responded in kind. We climbed steadily to the top of the neighborhood, watching a community football/*futsal* match with children playing. We met João, a local barber, who invited my son and I to have our hair cut. We had a sincere conversation in our broken Portuguese and English, learning that this was a thriving community, where being part of the neighborhood meant knowing who lived next door to you in an intimate and intertwined way. It was not a slum. This word is a cheap trope thrown around in the developed world, to poorly describe the inequity of access to certain resources and wealth. Santa Marta was cleaner than many of the U.S. neighborhoods we have visited, with an obvious communal pride. While the houses and buildings were made from makeshift materials, such as corrugated iron roofs and rendered walls, the insides of the houses we glimpsed were clean, cozy, and inviting. Nearly all were bright and colorful, with multi-patterned floral tiled floors and what seemed to be the essential appliance for all the residents of Santa Marta: a 55 in. big screen TV, where makeshift cables and satellite dishes piped in *The Beautiful Game:* live football. When we finally left, we were bidden a heartfelt farewell by João and his apprentice, and we walked down the mountain, taking with us an earnest, life-long appreciation for the people of Santa Marta.

These experiences became catalytic pivot-points; nexuses in the evolution of our family and the way in which we viewed the world as well as our place within it. It established firmly in our minds that all four of us being equal investors and architects in our family's ongoing story was how we would be able to continue to travel through life itself *together*, united in a partnership that has outlasted over a decade of travel, the rise and fall of many an entrepreneurial venture, our son and daughter both reaching adulthood, and even a global pandemic. For the obstacles we faced were no match to us being open, honest, and vulnerable with each other, to treating each other with the same respect no matter our ages or varying experiences, and to listening and working together. We always found the way in which we could keep moving forwards and prosper individually and as a family.

It also unequivocally reinforced our trust in the generosity and kindness of all humanity, especially when we choose to be sincere and authentic with each other. But most of all, it underscored the absolute value we were reaping from letting our children be our guides and mentors.

It was our son's persistence in the face of a very sticky situation, with borders to cross and accommodation to source and food to find on very little money, that inspired him at the age of 11 to get in touch with his own energetic integrity and superpower as a human being. From that moment in the Iguazu Bus Station onwards, his confidence grew, and he had the courage to take ownership of this vital aspect of our travels. This belief in himself manifested in him starting his own online travel concierge service, *Destinator Travel*, at 16. He created an inventive model of service where, when faced with the question of what to charge, he invited his clients to *pay what they thought his service was worth*. On average, this worked out to be around US$250 an hour for his services. Not bad for having created his own part-time job in his passion, especially considering that at the inception of the business, he would have been happy to offer his services for a mere US$25 an hour. More than all of this, however, Lalika created a way for himself to learn how to be a responsible entrepreneur, in a way that was fun for him, sustainable, and fair, where everyone felt they had achieved their best outcome.

A beautiful summer's day in Paris, relaxing on the grass at the Eiffel Tower and giving our feet a little rest after a morning exploring at the Louvre.

Excursion into the heart of Cheow Larn Lake in Thailand. We spent a weekend on a raft village with no electricity, hiking, kayaking, and boating through this incredible national park!

This chapter is a peek into what forged our foundations as a family, and for you to know that there is nothing to fear from facing the experiences that the world has to offer you, especially in these challenging times ahead. I seek to emphasize just how rich experiential learning is when you surrender desire for control and lean into the challenges that life presents you with. For it was only in fully embracing these tests that we found out just how dynamic and capable we are of overcoming, thriving, and integrating the multidimensional aspects of learning as a family.

It has even moved us to create something unique together today. Something we trust will inspire all families to realize their own power when they seek to question and embody the essence of who they are, together as a family.

This, for us, is the quintessence of the learning journey we face together as humanity at this fundamental juncture in our history. As humans, we seek a peaceful, coherent society, and our societies have always advocated for this from a top-down approach. But our journey has demonstrated to us that we will only find coherence and peace in society when we realize it within ourselves first. Only then can it extend to our families, and then to the world. Therefore, it is essential that we embrace and extend ourselves into every aspect of learning as it presents itself to us, no matter how weird or wonderful, in both the ultimate trust of our journey and the trust that everything will work out well.

Picnic at Machu Picchu.

Our home for the night: the parking lot at the base of the mighty Mount Hood in Oregon. Burritos baked for dinner in our little RV's oven before ascending the peak the next day.

This concept has been the underlying motivation for us to continue pushing the boundaries of our learning as a family in an ever-evolving way, and now, 12 years later, it has found new alignment in the formation of another learning adventure, a family venture created together by the four of us: *At Home In The World*.

At Home In The World is our attempt as a family to share what we have learnt and create a way in which we too can integrate our learning journey as a family, aligned with our daily lives, through a business that allows us to learn together, with and from many other families throughout the world. *At Home In The World Family Retreats* is just one aspect of this vision, where over the course of 10–14 days, we share our *familial framework for self-guided learning* through our in-person and online retreats. We take a journey together in how we can authentically deepen our connections to each other and the world, by asking those critical questions of ourselves, the ones that guide and teach us how we can be at home with ourselves, with our families, and in the world.

We are living in a world today where concerted forces try their best to influence us to realign our direction to *their* true north. This is infectious only if we choose to let it be. Listening to our inner voice, following our guides of intuition, trusting our choices, sticking to our convictions, and having faith in humanity will always see us emerge standing in our own sovereignty, and this is the place we all need to be, for it is where trust in our journey, no matter how wild the ride, will always deliver us to where everything works out, better than we could ever imagine.

Watching the sunset at Uluru on our open-ended road trip across Australia, the spontaneous adventure that sparked the inspiration for us to take our travels international.

11

The True Advantage of Worldschooling

Time

Alyson Long

I think I'm a pretty normal mother. I love my kids more than anything in this world and want what's best for them. I absolutely wanted the best possible education for them and the best childhood imaginable. To me that didn't involve the local school—it involved seeing the world.

We did, some 12 or so years ago, briefly enroll our firstborn in the local school. That was mostly because I didn't know of the alternatives. I didn't want him there, I wanted him home with me, but the concept of homeschooling was so outside my normal radar that it had barely crossed my mind at that point. I did what was expected of me, and what I was told.

A year or so in and it had become clear that this school wasn't enhancing anyone's life. I stomped in and hauled him out after a particularly unpleasant incident inflicted on him by another child. I had no clue how to proceed from there, but I knew neither of us would ever turn up at those school gates again.

We were living in a very small town in Far North Queensland and by chance, I happened to meet the only homeschooling family in town around this time. When you meet other homeschoolers

DOI: 10.4324/9781003267362-13

and find they're completely normal, you gain confidence. There were two mums now unhappy with the system and with just that little bit of support, I dove into homeschooling.

There were multiple hoops to jump through; I had to register as a homeschooler, submit learning plans, and reports. We did it—we got the official tick of approval from the government. The homeschooling paperwork wasn't hard but it was time-consuming and restrictive. The authorities wanted us to follow their strict curriculum and not have too many oddball ideas or our own, but still, we were approved.

If any mum is thrown into homeschooling as I was, they are more than likely to spend hours at the table with printed worksheets or online learning programs doing "school" at home. It didn't take me long to figure out that this is actually the worst way possible to do education.

I spotted that the two children (my younger child was just coming up to school age) learned most from what and who was around them. In some cases, this was the beach, the rainforest, or a TV presenter. It could be a fun book we read over and over, or an interesting adult friend. They were learning from their daily life.

We lived in a very small town and Australia is a huge country. There's not much scope for educational field trips. There were no museums or galleries, little of cultural interest, and very few other homeschoolers. I'm not from Australia. My kids were born in London and I remembered how much fun we used to have visiting London's amazing museums and going to the zoo every weekend. So I took them home for a holiday.

As we were in the UK I thought it only fair to pop over to Florida for them to visit Disney Florida too. That's not an easy trip to make from the southern hemisphere, but every kid deserves Disney. We were gone for about six weeks. That's the freedom you have when the kids aren't in school. I observed more learning. I loved spending all my time with them, showing them the things I knew they'd love. This is when our "worldschooling" idea was born.

Worldschooling as an alternative education method already existed, but I hadn't heard about it at that point. I was going to call it "travel schooling." I thought I'd had an original idea. My husband and I loved to travel. We met through travel and had already taken a gap year before having children. We thought that was how life had to be; you traveled and then had kids. We both wanted to take the boys traveling and show them the world's many wonders. We both wanted more family time and we saw no reason not to do it.

We left "home" in 2013 and were on the road for the next six years. We reverted to being British and my elder son eventually sat for the British IGCSE (International General Certificate of Secondary Education) exams during the lockdown. He passed with flying colors. These exams are open to kids of many nationalities and are recognized worldwide. No school attendance at all is required to sit the exams.

How did we educate on the road? It was a very unconventional, relaxed, eclectic form of homeschooling. The bulk of the boys' education has come about through conversation and their own explorations online. We had a lot of time to talk and to read. We once took them to Everest Base Camp; that's three weeks of conversation. You can "teach" a lot in three weeks. We talked about the mountains; how these high Himalayan peaks had once been on the bottom of the ocean, as evidenced by the pink salt and marine fossils they saw. We talked about climate along with the obvious erosion caused by deforestation and heavy donkey traffic. We noted that the people had come to Nepal from Tibet and looked at the crops they were able to grow up there. We considered diet. How do these people get vitamins? How do they conserve energy when fuel is so scarce? Our own health, acclimatization, fitness, and shortness of breath through lack of oxygen were noted daily. The physiology of adaptation to thin air, acute mountain sickness, and pulmonary edema is high-level biology that I covered in university. That thin air brought in physics and math. But our conversions drifted to all kinds of topics—whatever interested them, we talked about.

They also met a diverse collection of other humans to interact with and learn from. Not least, of course, the locals; Sherpa people who had summitted Everest as porters. They learned how hard that was and why these men (and a few Sherpa women) complete these trips when the risks are so high. They told us sobering stories from the earthquake. Our Sherpa friend was standing on the Khumbu glacier when that hit, with tourists that he had to protect from the resultant rockfall. Just being in such a place is so much more than being in a classroom.

Many people have called us unschoolers. I don't think we are because unschooling, by definition, has to be child-led. Although my boys were never forced to write essays, other than for home-school reports, I did take them to places and show them things that I thought they needed to know. I was guiding their learning to an extent. We were always searching out the historic sites and museums as well as diving deep into cultures, religions, food, and industry. We followed their passions too, of course. They both love ancient history and my elder son is currently taking A (Advanced) level history—the interest stuck.

This interest prompted them to ask us to take them to the sites of Ancient Greece and Egypt. The ruins of ancient civilizations along with museums, tours, guides, and the local people bring ancient history to life for the kids. Their interest gets deeper. These topics aren't on the normal school history curriculum, which is very disappointing. The parts of history that most kids find most interesting are totally disregarded in the exam system we went through. My younger son actually withdrew from his history class because he found the French Revolution so mind-numb-ingly boring. He'd expected history to be a lot more fun, as it had been when he was able to learn at the source. The Vietnam War and elements of WW2 were on the exam. What they'd seen living in Vietnam for six months or visiting the Somme Battlefields was undoubtedly useful. They had stood in the trenches, knew the landscape, and saw the cemeteries in France. They could better visualize the reality of trench warfare.

Of course, at the time, we'd discussed the war, how it started, who was involved, and how it ended. Those seeds had already been planted. It was also useful in studying the war poets in their eventual English literature classes—so many related to suffering in the trenches and the tragic consequences of war. In Vietnam, we toured the Cu Chi Tunnels, visited the DMZ (Demilitarized Zone), saw the Ho Chi Minh trail along with the war museums. They already knew how Vietnam had been devastated by bombings. They knew how resilient the Vietnamese people are, as witnessed by how our friends in Hoi An just shrugged off another flood. It happens most years. After three days living on upper floors the waters receded, they cleared up, and went back to business as usual, smiling and laughing throughout. Our landlady joked that "now they have big swimming pool" as she text messaged me from above a muddy brown torrent. They also knew that the Vietnamese are some of the nicest, kindest people on the planet. They could relate to the era better because of their experiences. They could empathize. They knew that the people must have suffered for years with only rice and cassava to eat. The Vietnamese are incredible cooks; these wartime rations weren't the great Vietnamese food my boys were eating every day. The country is still littered with bomb craters. Neighboring Laos was bombed heavily too; live devices are still being found to this day as evidenced by the amputees, the kids in wheelchairs, and the explosion-blinded young man we met at an amputee aid center. Not only blind, the bomb took his hands too. This incredibly diverse general knowledge that the children picked up will mostly never be tested by the system, but that doesn't make this knowledge any less valuable.

We traveled to 50 or so countries, but eventually COVID-19 arrived and we were stranded. Just sitting in the house seemed pointless so we enrolled them in an online school to pass the time in some useful way. It all worked out just fine. They were no more "ahead" nor "behind" than any of the other kids and they kind of enjoyed it. It was something to do during a very long, boring, lockdown. In some areas, notably geography and history, their knowledge was occasionally better than their teacher's. They certainly didn't, and don't, want to go to a "real" school. They're undecided as yet on university and that's just fine.

Worldschooling does not prepare kids to sit exams. You can't go straight from a travel lifestyle to an exam hall and expect your kids to pass. There is a certain skill set required for every exam, and exam technique is something best taught by teachers. The kids must at least have seen previous papers and know what's expected of them in their answers. In our experience, these skills didn't take long to acquire at all. It took a few terms, with English being the most troublesome in terms of exam technique. In some instances, these exam skills were simple things, such as always showing work in math exams. My boys just wrote the answers when they could complete a question in their heads. They had no clue that they had to record every mathematical step of the way to gain full marks. The breadth of knowledge they've acquired from such extensive travel is, of course, not on the tests. Exams aren't compulsory for most of us. I would argue that they're not essential nor necessarily important, but we ended up taking that route purely because of the pandemic.

My younger son taught himself to read and write because he wanted to label his Minecraft creations. In homeschooling and unschooling circles you'll often hear that kids can teach themselves skills like that. I didn't really believe it until I saw it happen. Not all kids will, of course. Some kids today still come out of the school system functionally illiterate. I did "teach" them biology, and a lot of sciences. That came about mostly through conversation and questions, not tests and memorization. We did, at times, use online learning tools, workbooks, textbooks, and conventional "school" type methods. I did get them into crosswords and word searches. Ultimately, though, our learning occurred by living.

Worldschooling Advantages

Overall this worldschooling path brought us many advantages. For one, we have more family time, and we have no teen issues. We all get on well. My teens enjoy spending time and traveling with us. We've never fought over curfews nor worried where they are and we're still all friends. Our lives are more shared, and our memories are all shared. I think spending so much time together doing interesting things has made our lives more intertwined and we've avoided the child and parent division that is created by school life being separate to family life.

Dad's busy and unconventional chef hours made him a very absent parent in their early years. He even had to work every Christmas day. A chef's working hours do not fit around school hours well; he rarely saw his very small children. As bloggers, today, we are able to fit work around life, not the other way round. We built a global business that fully funded our travels. It is incredibly fulfilling to work for yourself, be your own boss, and help the next generation of travelers—millions of them—all around the globe. Working online means that we can work wherever we are. All we need is a phone, laptop, and a Wi-Fi connection.

This lifestyle also brought us freedom to go or be anywhere whenever we wanted. If we'd had enough of cities we could head for the mountains. If we needed a food fix, back we'd go to India or Thailand. In winter we could choose to ski or head somewhere warmer. We could visit friends and family around the globe or be strangers in a new land. Whatever we needed at that time, we could usually engineer. With the ability to travel anywhere, we also had the time to develop any skills we needed to use. When my son decided to learn to scuba dive, we were able to dedicate a week to it. There was no school or work getting in the way. I wanted my boys to be able to ski, so we spent winters near the very affordable ski slopes of Romania. We didn't need to ask permission to take time off to ski on the days when the skies were blue and there was fresh powder.

Skill-building also coincides with volunteer work—yet another advantage of having time. One of the kids has spent months of his life helping pick up marine debris from beaches. This isn't just volunteering, it's a scientific research project that he's heavily involved in, along with marine biologists and other conservation specialists. He knows where those plastics come from and which currents put them there. He's volunteering, having fun, getting fit, seeing remote places, and learning at the same time. Projects like this also look great on a young person's CV. There's no way a school timetable would have afforded him the time to be involved.

We also had time to test ourselves and build self-esteem through triumph over adversity. One of the boys once said that they could do anything because he'd been to Everest Base Camp. Aside from cold, altitude, and three weeks of walking, conditions are tough up there. They've also survived three winters in Romania with just a wood stove for heat. These kids will take on most things without flinching.

Another advantage of worldschooling is developing fitness and the opportunity to take part in activities we loved. The kids are proficient skiers and masters of trekking. Three of us are scuba divers. Our preferred sports are running, cycling, and Ironman triathlon; we've participated in all of these things all over the world. There are no team sports on the list. I was forced to take part in team sports in school and loathed every second. My husband competes in extreme Ironman and ultrarunning events at a high level. I don't see why team sports are perceived as necessary when they actually turn a lot of kids off exercise in school.

The travel lifestyle kept me much fitter than the sedentary existence lockdown forced. I gained 22 lbs. That's an obvious lifestyle change. My diet was also much worse the minute I returned to a western country from Asia. I've since lost that weight through putting structured exercise back into my life, which wasn't nearly as necessary on the road. Had my husband been still working a regular job, there would be no way he would have been able to take time off to compete globally. The kids never had to sit at desks; they were free to move, or not, as they chose.

Mentally and emotionally, we benefited too. We have diverse friends of all nationalities and from all levels of society. My boys don't see adults as different; they see more people to interact with, or not. We're all introverts and don't need a lot of people around us. They have buddies in London, Romania, Vietnam. They know Sherpas, seamstresses, and a lot of travel professionals. My elder son has even traveled with me as my business associate, covering a headhunter tribe in Borneo deep in the jungle. Later we toured the sights of Bhutan with a group. He loved both experiences and had a position of responsibility as my videographer and drone pilot. At one point they were even friends with a stage magician and his family. They've met a lot of very interesting people, some good, some bad. Many are entrepreneurs or in some way less than conventional.

We benefited from having no routine, no day-to-day grind. Every day could be different if we chose it to be. We had a much lighter chore load and fewer possessions to worry about. I didn't even need to cook in Asia, we ate out paying a dollar or so for healthy, fresh, street food, the same as the locals eat. We never had to wash bedding or clean our rooms; that's the beauty of paying to stay in hotels and guest houses. Nobody ever needed to be up, washed and dressed, and ready for work or school. We did have quite a few very early flights and buses though; the kids know how to be flexible.

No school meant no bullying. Bullying in school reduces self-belief and robs kids of confidence. Teachers and kids can be bullies. I strongly reject any suggestion that bullying is good for kids and helps them "toughen up." We wouldn't accept this kind of situation as adults so why should kids be forced to endure it? Likewise, being bottom of the class or bad at sports also knocks confidence. What if they're not the most popular, what if they are ridiculed for some physical "defect" like acne, or having the wrong color hair? My kids have never experienced any of this, nor have they ever been that bully.

Ultimately, we had time and freedom. We had freedom to learn about anything we chose. The school curriculum is limited and homework takes up time outside of school. We have learned about things way outside of what's taught in school. We spent a lot of time on Thai history and the movements of peoples in Southeast Asia. We learned some Romanian, although I learned a lot more than the boys. My kids are not the natural language sponges people make kids out to be. We learned how to survive freezing conditions with no modern conveniences. We learned about subsistence farming through living cheek by jowl with amazing people. World religions were an unavoidable thing to learn. You can't travel and not learn about the religions you encounter along the way. The boys learned to make videos, to stream, and become YouTubers; these are real-world income generators and they've had the time to grow these skills. Likewise, they've had endless time to read the books they wanted to read. Those books include classical Greek works. I can't tell you how much they hate some of the curriculum books for English Literature. Their favorite, by far, is *Macbeth*. *Of Mice and Men* and *The Curious Incident of the Dog in The Nighttime* have been dissected and shredded until any possible enjoyment has been removed.

Through traveling, though, we have learned a greater awareness of how things are in many parts of the world. Can a child in a classroom really visualize how life looks for people in other countries? Are their perceptions accurate, or reflections of a biased media? It's important to know the realities of the world. Somebody once said to me, "Why would I want to go to some third world country?" My kids could give him plenty of reasons.

Worldschooling Tips

◆ Worldschooling can be achieved in many ways, but obviously, it must involve travel. We believe that the more countries, climates, and cultures you can visit, the better. Pick places that are as diverse as possible to expose your children to as much of the world as you can. Travel as long as you can, as far as you can, as wide as you can.

◆ If you have eventual exams in mind (we didn't) know what's on the curriculum. For instance, if glaciers are in the geography exam, take them to see one, and to see some U-shaped and hanging valleys. If there is to be a question on the Vietnam War, go to the Ho Chi Minh trail, Cu Chi tunnels, and the War Remnants Museum. Go and see Uncle Ho embalmed in Hanoi. For ancient history, you'll want to visit Egypt, Greece, Angkor Wat, Tikal, and maybe even Mesopotamia! For science, head to the Kennedy Space Center, the Smithsonian, the museums of natural history, and the hands-on science museums. Art is a wonderful thing to study through travel; compare Arabic art with Dali in Spain, Van Gogh in Amsterdam, and traditional Aboriginal art and cave paintings in Australia. Then consider languages. If you need to become fluent in a second language, it's much faster to learn when you are fully immersed. Spanish-speaking countries in the Americas, in particular, are good for this, as in most other places in the world there is no language barrier for English speakers.

◆ Let your children read constantly, but also allow them to use computers. We never had handheld devices or phones until they were older. They read on their Kindles for hours on buses, planes, and at airports. They used laptops only when we were in our lodgings. Online skills are vital in today's world; kids need these skills. I earn a living online and my kids are often the ones I ask if I have a technical problem. They also need to read widely. Being able to buy and download new books in seconds was gold. They are both still big readers today. Kids in school wouldn't have the time to do this.

◆ Really know your kids. This is essential. Don't put them in situations that will make them uncomfortable. Know what they will enjoy and do pretty much everything with them in mind. If you're going to successfully live a travel lifestyle, your kids have to enjoy it. If that means hours on playgrounds or frequent ice cream breaks, so be it. My kids have no interest in beaches. Neither do I. Beach relaxation would have turned them right off the whole plan. Likewise, one of them is quite sensitive; we skipped the killing fields and avoided lepers. It was too much for him back then. You can't always do what you want to do when you're traveling with kids. Reduce risk too—there was no more traveling on the roof of the bus in India once the kids came along. I'm sure they would have loved it though!

◆ You'll have to be pretty much self-contained in terms of social need. There are other humans around constantly, but you're unlikely to strike up real friendships in a transient travel lifestyle. A lot of traveling families arrange social get-togethers and play dates with complete strangers on the road because they are worried their kids don't get to "socialize." We never engineered these but we went along to a few. They weren't something the kids, nor we, particularly enjoyed. On the road, you are in society every day, fully immersed, constantly surrounded by people. Often too many people! Socialization is concerned with acquiring the customs and beliefs of your society.

We aimed to be "socialized" into a global society, not any particular local one. Certainly not the limited number of kids, all from the same places, all born in the same year, that a classroom provides. That said, we did make quite a few lifelong friends during these years, of all ages and nationalities. This can only happen when you're in one spot for an extended period. Close friendships require time, and yes, online friends are real friends. That's something we've tried and tested many times over.

◆ Have fun! Don't see your travels as purely educational. Enjoy yourselves. Let your kids have an absolute ball. Don't drag them around museums they have no interest in. Allow them to linger when they find those they love. Follow their interests, follow their needs, make this adventure something they love. There is no need at all to separate the "educational" from the fun. There is learning to be had in absolutely every location, just open your eyes a little wider to see it and answer the questions they will inevitably ask.

12

From Surfing to Schooling

There Is More to Homeschool Than Worksheets

Robyn Robledo

I never thought I would be an unschooler. As an overachiever myself, school always came easy and getting straight A's throughout my own schooling journey made me feel proud and confident, but not necessarily happy. I started my homeschooling journey back in 2002. My oldest was three years old and we lived in one of the most affluent cities in America, Coronado, California, where most people sent their kids to preschool at age three.

It was not a good fit for my son. While it was only twice a week from 8:30 to 1:30, by the time 11 AM rolled around, I would be getting a phone call from the office saying I needed to pick Danny up because he was crying in the corner sucking his thumb and holding his blanket. It only took a few weeks of this before I realized this was not the path for him.

At the time, I was also running a gymnastics facility and was teaching some homeschool families who I admired for how kind and well behaved their kids were. While I didn't really start teaching my 3-year-old anything at that point, that was the moment I decided to homeschool my own children.

DOI: 10.4324/9781003267362-14

Over the years, as I had more kids, I chose a very structured format. Since I was running a gymnastics facility, I needed to work in the afternoons. In addition, I always had a baby or toddler that needed naps, so a structured homeschooling environment helped me maintain my sanity and establish rules, boundaries, and expectations in our household.

Tip: If you are just starting your homeschool journey, write down your intention and expectation. This can make all the difference in loving or hating the homeschool life.

It was great for many years to teach math, science, history, and English. In fact, we had a huge 10-foot chalkboard and cute little flip desks for each kid that made our classroom feel official and fun. I was the type of teacher who spent every Sunday outlining exactly the lessons I would teach and would print out a syllabus, which was detailed in 1five-minute chunks, for the entire week. I'd set monthly goals, give grades, and made sure they knew exactly what was expected of them.

But by 2010, when Tatiana was born, and the rest of my kids were 11, 9, 6, and 2 years old, respectively, I was getting bored with the homeschooling routine. I wanted to just have fun. I had had enough of being indoors until 1 PM and then having to go teach gymnastics. I wanted to be outdoors, playing with the kids, enjoying life, and so, I gradually spent less and less time doing school curriculum and spent more time going to the park, the beach, and on field trips.

Once Tatiana was a year old and finished breast feeding, my desire for adventure was on fire. We had recently begun camping, something we hadn't done in the first 1 five years of our marriage and my husband, Victor, had never even done in his youth. We were spending our weekends riding ATV's in the desert or camping at the beach and I had decided to pick up a surfboard and learn to surf. Instead of the lazy mornings of cartoons, breakfast, and getting started with math at 9 AM, our homeschool days looked more like 7 AM wake-up calls with me screaming, "Hurry up and get dressed, we're going to the beach!"

Surfing Changed Everything

Going to the beach and park was nice and we still did a little traditional school in the form of math lessons, history, science, and English. But in 2012, I did something else that would dramatically change the trajectory of our life. I signed up for yoga teacher training. Not that yoga training is anything special. In fact, there are more yoga teachers than lawyers in California. But it was dramatic in that it was the first time for me, as a mom, to choose to do something selfish. Something just for me, myself, and my self-growth.

There was an underlying feeling of fear, guilt, and shame for taking time away from being a mom but it was only for two weeks and so I let those emotions settle into the back of my mind and allowed the experience of self-discovery to be in the spotlight. I didn't stop with yoga though. On my way to or from the yoga trainings, I'd stop at the beach some days and paddle out on my surfboard. I'd been playing around increasingly with surfing when we'd go camping on the weekends and was eager to break through the slow and difficult learning curve in hopes of someday being able to call myself *a surfer*.

And break through I did. It wasn't long before I was not only a surfer, but also a yoga instructor, rock climber, and mountain biker. While the new identity sounded cool (and super Cali) it wasn't the reason I started chasing adventure with passion and persistence. It was the addiction to my newfound sense of self. The new "I" that I was embodying. In the silence between sets, in the stillness of just my breath, in the focus on the rock wall or down hilling over roots, I was discovering that I wasn't just a mom. I was so much more. *And if I was so much more, then my kids were so much more too.*

Tip: Consider your identities outside of mom and outside of your career. What do you enjoy? Make time for these activities. What about your children? What are their identities? Talk to them about these.

I had to help them discover who they were. All this time spent on math, science, history, English—for what? What good is it to be able to memorize facts if we feel lost or disconnected from our true selves?

These types of changes never happen overnight. And it's rarely one discipline or action that creates a new result. In this case, the curiosity of learning to surf led to a curiosity of discovering the self. This then led to a curiosity for travel.

Isn't Life Wonder-Full?

I used to stand on the beach staring at the ocean wondering what it might feel like to surf, what it would be like to take a vacation in an RV, what it would be like to be a mom. I'd drive through the familiar roads of San Diego wondering what other parts of the U.S. look like. Wonder is a beautiful thing and the few people who are brave enough to pause reality and chase that wonder, know that the best moments in life all started with a simple thought.

Travel Opened a New Classroom Door

In 201five, we were renting a house on the beach in Coronado. Between early morning surf sessions, playing soccer in the grass at the park, and still making time for some traditional schoolwork, we were happy. We were busy, but not so busy that we couldn't lie in the grass and watch the clouds float by or hop on our bikes and explore the neighborhood. If the landlord hadn't wanted her house back, we probably would've continued on in the same predictable pattern following the same daily routine.

Our routines and attachment to predictability create a wall that binds us to the grass we know and keeps us blind to the possibilities of the unknown. We moved out of that house April Fool's Day 201five, but we didn't move into a new house. Instead, we moved our family of seven into a 30 ft. Class C RV.

At first, we said it would just be temporary. A practical move to save money. We thought we'd do it for five months and then find a new house to rent. But in those five months walls came down, I saw a lot of grass, and I was filled with way more wonder. In those five months, we traveled through Arizona, Utah, Colorado, Northern California, Oregon, and Washington. We hiked dozens of new trails and explored mountains, deserts, oceans, lakes, and everything in between. We went to the Grand Canyon, the Rocky Mountains, Yosemite National Park, Mount St. Helens, Mount Rainier, and the Olympic National Park.

Besides the lessons, travel in general was teaching; the days spent exploring the outdoors, the kids learning from junior ranger books, reading trail signs, and playing in nature were way more educational than the studies they had been doing with textbooks. This new hands-on approach to learning was squeezing out the old ways and before long I found myself saying, "We don't need to do school today. Just go outside and play. Get dirty. Explore. Figure things out."

Tip: Get out of your regular routine for a month, a week, or even a day. Take a trip. Go hike somewhere new. Take a risk to do something you and your family have never done before. Afterwards, reflect together!

When September rolled around and we were supposed to find a rental and go back to our ordinary life, my husband looked at me and said, "You are so happy, why don't we just keep living like this?" We kept living in the RV in San Diego (because we had to make money and our business was there) and so we didn't travel much.

Our school days were still mixed in with surfing but I still used workbooks and traditional curriculum as the backbone of our homeschooling curriculum. In June 2016, we boarded a plane with just backpacks (and surfboards, rock climbing gear, and tents) and flew to Europe for six months in what would be the nail in the coffin for me to abandon that antiquated model of education and embrace what I call SOUL schooling and what others refer to as unschooling.

Walking Is Man's Best Medicine

We spent a lot of our time in Europe hiking. A beautiful thing happens when you hike; your mind begins to wander. You get lost in thought. You have quiet space to reflect. I used to tell my husband that homeschooling isn't about what I'm teaching them, it's the time and space I'm allowing for them to notice and express their thoughts. I can't imagine how much thought, emotion, and feeling gets lost or forgotten from the minds of our youth when they are forced to sit still and listen for hours a day.

Ask any homeschooling parent and they will say that their kids never stop talking. It's incredible how much kids have to say when provided a space for expression. Parents need to respect their inquisitive nature (without losing sanity). This is one of the best ways to nurture your child's development and create a springboard to their success— *especially if you define success as happiness built around intrinsic values.*

Hiking in Europe meant there was a lot of talking. Tons of ideas and questions were being bounced off one another in a creative attempt to make sense of a beautiful yet confusing world. This Socratic form of learning paved the way to even more time spent pursuing the answers to these questions and following ideas down a rabbit hole, and almost no time for traditional school subjects.

At the time, my oldest daughter Gabi was 15 and loved photography. In addition, she had great researching skills and so we decided to start a blog together. We didn't really have a clue what that would entail but we started by documenting some of the travel and uploading pictures along the way. She was passionate about it and that alone made much more sense to me for her to pursue then learning calculus or physics or whatever she was supposed to be memorizing in high school.

This was also the first time in all my years of homeschooling that my husband was around all the time. For this 6-month trip, we had saved up enough money that he didn't need to work and could just be a parent. He took over the schooling with the younger two and spent hours a day reading about dogs or whatever else Jiraiya was obsessed with at the time. Tatiana was only six and couldn't do a lot of the harder hikes, so she'd stay back in the RV with Victor and they'd use paper plates and duct tape to make arts and crafts for hours.

That was their "schooling" that year and it was amazing! They were happy, creative, and most importantly, they loved having their daddy's attention all day. The older kids and I were happy exploring and challenging ourselves. My oldest son, who was 17, spent his days writing books and eventually self-published them on Amazon.

Isabelle, my middle child who was 12 at the time, had always been drawn to creative projects. While traveling, she'd spend hours a day drawing and looking back I see how this creative outlet paved the way for her entrepreneurial spirit. As each child had more time to pursue their own interests and develop their passions, it was becoming very apparent to me how different they thought and how different their brains processed information.

In this unschooling approach, no one struggled. There were no tears learning math or nagging about writing essays. Once they found something that excited them, they'd lose themselves in it for hours. I'd often have to drag them away from their projects so we could go play and explore. (After all, that's why we were traveling!)

Whether it was writing a book, editing photos, drawing, learning about every species of dog, or making duct tape kittens, each of them was eager to engage in learning and doing. It didn't take me long to think...*this* is what makes people successful. Desire. Motivation. Persistence. So I challenged them to do it more.

It became a rule in our family that you don't have to do school as long as you are pursuing a creative goal. It doesn't have to make money per se, but it has to challenge your mind, develop a skill, and be something you are passionate about. No video games or distractions that make you act like a zombie.

We finished our Europe trip, went back to California to work, but didn't return to the old ways of doing school. If we weren't traveling, then I'd still expect the younger two to do math and Wordly Wise each day. After all, I still feel strongly about needing a base of logic and there's no simpler way to teach logic then making sure kids understand that $2 + 2 = 4$.

There's also a certain amount of organization and discipline that comes from kids knowing how to line up and solve math equations. But even this has room for interpretation and should be decided upon based on how your child learns and where you see their spirit thriving.

Teaching to Your Child's Personality

Switching from a structured homeschooling environment to passion-driven learning with an ever changing backyard would have been enough to raise happy, healthy kids who had the skill set to succeed in the world. But then, we stumbled upon personality types and took our homeschooling to a whole new level.

We were hiking Fox Glacier in New Zealand when Isabelle first mentioned The Myers Briggs Type Indicator. I was fascinated as she was explaining the letters and jumped on my phone when we got to our Airbnb to take the test and find out what I was. At first, it was purely entertaining and gave us something to talk about over the next few months of traveling through the South Island and later in Bali. But eventually, it changed even more how I looked at education and how I defined success.

Seeing how cognitive function and personality type varied from child to child made me excited to help nurture each kid in different ways. I found myself encouraging my SJ child to do more workbooks and my NE child to talk and plan out his crazy ideas. On top of that, we learned about the Enneagram and this helped me understand why consistency was so important for one child while fun, achievement, or research was the driving force for others.

Tip: Discover yours and your child's personality types, both MBTI and Enneagram. We have videos on our App, *Nomads With A Purpose*, which can help you understand how to test and integrate these results.

The Future of Homeschooling

I know, it sounds like spiritual juju and you might be thinking how an internal energy hub has anything to do with, say, learning math. If you think the world we have lived in for the past 80 years is going to continue in this fashion, you haven't been paying close attention. The world is changing and changing fast. The job force is changing and so, the necessity of college is also changing.

Not to say colleges don't love accepting homeschool kids, it's just that the entire *system* is changing from the education we knew to something completely different. The narrative of "get good grades in school so you can get into a good college and get a good job and then in 30 years you get to retire and start enjoying life" is changing.

Now, more than ever, our kids are going to need emotional resiliency that comes from understanding who they are and what makes them happy. Those who have this self-awareness are going to have the ability to create jobs that play to their unique perspective of life and individual talents. Without it, I think our kids will feel lost. In fact, I think that's what we are seeing right now.

I taught gymnastics to kids for 20 years. In that time, I have witnessed the degradation of the family. The need for a two-income family was growing. Parents were exhausted from working too much. They didn't have the energy or time to give to their kids. Parents would sign their kids up for classes purely because they needed a break. The kids just wanted to be listened to and hugged. It wasn't healthy.

Life's a little hard right now. It can feel confusing and overwhelming, but we need this shift. If I could give a new parent one piece of advice it would be to prioritize time over stuff. It's too easy to get caught in the scarcity mindset trap.

What if my kid isn't on the All Star team?
What if they aren't top of their class?
What if they don't always have the latest video game or newest fashions?

The whole thing is a trap to make you feel unworthy—nothing is ever enough. But it's a lie. You already have everything you need to nurture your child to an amazing life. My husband and I have a motto we live by when raising our kids: "Be Who You Want Your Kids To Be." For the most part, if you can slow down enough to be aware of and aligned with who you are and the example you are living by, then the homeschooling part is easy.

All you have to do is slow down, listen to them, go for a walk, ask questions, share your thoughts, allow for imperfection, trial and error, and trust that there is a force out there much greater than status quo. When the goal is better health, more memories, and a deeper connection, you will stop looking for validation externally and can easily stay aligned to the intrinsic values that motivated you to have kids in the first place.

I personally value research, resourcefulness, and rhetoric over reading, writing, and arithmetic. As an Enneagram 8, INTJ type, I want my kids to be capable, self-responsible, and to constantly challenge themselves. But those are my values. It's important that you know yours.

Homeschooling is about creating an environment for self-growth, self-love, and self-exploration. Yes, they need to read, write, and crunch a few numbers, but what good are those skills if they don't know who they are and why they are here in the first place? You can choose to make yourself blue in the face telling them what they should do or you can create space for them to discover and choose who they want to be.

Know Your Intention

I live in an RV, drive an old truck, and own only a few pairs of shoes. But I travel the world with my family, have a loving husband, and my kids are happy and pursing their passions. For me, that was my intention. I didn't care about having millions of dollars, my kids going to college, or any status.

I wanted connection with my body, my soul, my loved ones, and nature. I wanted to raise kids who were capable, and knew and loved themselves, were resilient, and had a willingness to pursue their passions and persist until they found their purpose. Some will achieve this by 20, some may take until 30, but I do know that this formula works and that the end result is what we wanted from our parenting journey from the beginning, to raise happy, healthy kids.

Interlude

Mindfulness for Home Educators

Hunter Clarke-Fields

As a home educator, you've chosen to dedicate many resources and hours to your child. You are staying close and will be there for their wins and struggles, their emotional ups and downs. What's absolutely vital and non-negotiable in this situation? Taking care of *you*.

As parents, you may have been taught by culture that to be a "good" parent you must sacrifice yourself, but in fact, this is a recipe for burnout and resentment. To truly show up for your child, you need to meet your own needs on a daily basis. Your child is depending on you to be a model of healthy adulthood. They need a parent who is able to stay calm in the face of stormy emotions. They need a parent who is emotionally stable and available, firm yet flexible, joyful, and relatively stress free.

So how do we become that parent? First, taking care of your basic needs must be a priority: get enough sleep, eat well, get fresh air, and exercise. Once those priorities are established, I encourage you to anchor yourself through your home-education journey with mindfulness practices. Why mindfulness? Because we all inherited a nervous system that is wired for reactivity— and when we are reactive, we are at our worst with our children. Our stress response leads us to loud, frightening reactions to our children's behavior. Mindfulness meditation is an accessible,

DOI: 10.4324/9781003267362-15

research-proven practice that can steady the stress response and give you more equanimity when responding to your child.

Mindfulness meditation is intentionally training our attention to be in the present moment, non-reactive, with a sense of non-judgmental curiosity. Mindfulness meditation has many benefits and effectively zero negative side effects. Researchers from Johns Hopkins University found 47 studies that show that mindfulness meditation can help ease psychological stresses from anxiety, depression, and chronic pain. More research has shown that it increases positive emotion, increases social connection and emotional intelligence and, importantly, improves your ability to regulate your emotions (this is just what parents need!).

I've seen all of these benefits in my own life and in the lives of my clients. Put simply, practicing mindfulness gives us a sense of equanimity and the grounding we need to parent well.

How does it work? Mindfulness meditation can significantly change how reactive our brains are over time. After an 8-week course of mindfulness practice, MRI scans show that the brain's "fight or flight" centers, the amygdalae, actually appear to shrink. Not only that, but as the amygdalae shrink, the prefrontal cortex (the area associated with more complex brain functions such as awareness, concentration, empathy, and decision-making)– becomes thicker. This means that meditation is physically changing the brain (wow) in a way that weakens our reactivity!

How to Practice Mindfulness

How do you practice mindfulness? You deliberately focus your attention on what is happening in the here and now, aiming to be *more* attentive to the present moment rather than distracted. You practice noticing what's going on moment to moment, within you and around you, with kindness and curiosity—*non-judgmentally*.

Choose a regular time each day to establish the habit of sitting meditation. It's lovely to wake up a few minutes early and start your day with mindfulness practice. It sets the tone for the rest of the day. However, many people practice in the evening, and parents in particular often have to be creative about finding those few minutes. Whether it's morning, lunch break, or nap time, try to find the same time each day. Your goal is to make meditation a habit as regular as brushing your teeth.

Ease your way in, starting with short meditations, then build up to more time, eventually aiming for twenty minutes a day.

Practice: Sitting Mindfulness Meditation

Find a quiet time and place. Sit up tall on a chair or cushion. Sit upright, but relaxed. Be comfortable! You can even meditate in a recliner. Either cup your hands, letting your thumbs touch, or simply rest them on your legs. Set a timer so you don't have to worry about the time.

Close your eyes fully or leave them at half-mast. Bring your attention to your breath and your body. Let your mind be spacious and your heart be kind and soft. Feel your breath at your belly or your nose. Let your breath be natural. Notice each in-breath and notice each out-breath. Say to yourself: "breathing in" as you breathe in and "breathing out" as you breathe out.

If focusing on your breath makes you feel the opposite of calm, instead focus on the sounds you hear or the sense of your body touching the chair or floor.

Expect your mind to wander right away. That's normal! The goal is not to stop your thoughts, but to train your attention. The goal is to spend more time in the present moment and less time lost in distraction. Label your thoughts "thinking" if you want, then return your attention to your breath. Do this again and again, and again, and again. Each time you discover your mind has wandered is an opportunity to do a "rep" and build that mindfulness muscle. Even if you think you are doing this badly, it still works.

Meditation thrives on practice and a kind approach. If you do this simple practice every day, you will gradually become more grounded and aware.

Your meditation practice can put you back in control of your mind, rather than being pushed around by its automatic reactions. It will increase your self-awareness and help you to come back to the present moment. When you can come back to the present and see clearly, many anxieties and fears drop away, and you will be less reactive.

Deciding to educate your child at home is a big journey. Make sure you are prepared for it with a steady heart, mind, and nervous system. Plus, far more than toys or lessons, your child needs *you*—the authentic you underneath all of the stress and reactivity—with less tension and more presence and ease. Your ability to be fully present will naturally start to soothe your child, helping them feel seen, heard, and accepted. Zen master Thich Nhat Hanh sums this up beautifully:

When you love someone, the best thing you can offer is your presence. How can you love if you are not there?

I Am

Isabelle Robledo

(17-year-old homeschooler)

Every day I wake up
and I stare at my reflection
Trying to figure out what I truly am
And what of it is just projection

I've never known who I am,
If I'm emptiness at my core
And I've searched the world, end to end
To discover if I am more

People say I'm Funny
so maybe Funny is who I am
My family says I'm Beautiful
And astrology says I'm the Ram

I write these things on my mirror
To memorize what makes me, me
And as the world tells more of what I am
My own reflection gets harder to see

They say that I'm a mindfulness coach
A musician, an artist, their best friend

DOI: 10.4324/9781003267362-16

They give me all these "I am" labels
Then I never see them again

I have no more room on the mirror
To write who I am
Panicking that I'm back where I started
I'm no more than a shallow scam

I look back up at the mirror
And see a sliver of my own eyes
That was the moment I realized
I had woven a web of lies

"Who I am" isn't outside of me
It never was from the start
It's not a label, a title,
a personality type, or a chart

I'm frustrated with myself
At all the time I spent living in 2D
I find a brick on the floor
And throw it at what I thought defined me

The mirror shatters and falls
With a loud crash and a sigh
Gone are all the things I thought defined me
Destroyed is the web of lies

It felt painful to throw that brick
To destroy my perfect identity
But now with the mirror gone
All there is left is me

I may be funny,
Beautiful
Talented
A coach

And kind,
Aggressive
Giving
A Peacemaker
ISTP MBTI

But that's not who I am

"I am" is a simple term
Meant to be left as it is
Not "I am a teen, a barista
or the middle child of five kids"

"Who I am" cannot be defined
It's simply my existences' core
It's the ground that I can return to
When people don't tell me who I am anymore

"I am" is my reminder
When I start to feel alone
"I am" is my mantra
To remind me I'm home

I am more than what you think of me
Because I am indescribable
So don't try to control me
with your dumb and phony title

"I AM" that is all
And what a relief too
Because adding to the end of that statement
Will only take you further from the true you

"You are" that is all
"I am" and that's all I have to be
Don't tell yourself anything different
Break that mirror and you'll see

Conclusion

Katie Rybakova Mathews

Not every quilt or blanket qualifies as a tapestry. Tapestries are usually decorative woven fabrics, their threads stitched together to conceal warps. The imperfections of each thread weave together to create a beautiful image. Whether draped around your shoulders or hanging from a wall, a tapestry symbolizes union—an intricate and complex representation of the human collective's many gifts and talents.

When I first started collecting chapters for this book, I was amazed by the amount of homeschooling families who wanted to share their story. It was not because they thought they "did it right," but rather because they wanted to contribute a thread in the diverse and beautiful tapestry that makes up the larger home-schooling community. They wanted to be heard. They wanted to remind the larger *education* community that homeschooling is a legitimate—if not better—way to educate our youth.

In teacher preparation, a common term used is differentiation. As a teacher educator, my classes revolve around the idea of differentiating instruction—in other words, making sure that as a teacher, we connect the content that we teach to all of our students in a way that is motivating, engaging, and accessible. It is a lifelong challenge for teachers of all kinds to do this. Rather than viewing homeschooling as an alternative form of education or a "pulling

DOI: 10.4324/9781003267362-17

out" of traditional public schooling, let us visualize a future where homeschooling is simply another form of differentiation. What works for one child may not work for another, and it is far easier to differentiate when working in small ratios of student-to-teacher. Homeschooling—and homeschoolers—are not to be feared as the "other," but rather embraced as simply an option on the long continuum of learning. We are differentiating instruction not by changing our pedagogy but changing our setting. We are simply using a different thread on the same tapestry. Homeschoolers are not to be feared. *Homeschooling* is not to be feared.

This book symbolizes a tapestry. It blankets my shoulders with the stories of those who have come before me in this journey of homeschooling and lifelong learning. Whether in nature or down the road less traveled, take this woven tapestry with you on your journey. Regardless of where you are in that journey, and regardless of how you have chosen to educate your children, let this tapestry warm and comfort you. When you are ready—when you have climbed the proverbial mountain—you too will contribute to this growing tapestry. For now, let us take it a step at a time, reminded that for every challenging moment there is an equally beautiful outcome. Trust the journey, and you'll reach the peak.

It's a heck of a view.